Family Matters...in

Rhyme

A COLLECTION OF STORIES AND POEMS

Johnnie Walker

ISBN 978-1-64670-413-2 (Paperback)
ISBN 978-1-64670-414-9 (Digital)

Covenant Books, Inc.
11661 Hwy 707
Murrells Inlet, SC 29576
www.covenantbooks.com

THIS BOOK IS DEDICATED TO MY DAUGHTER—
KEYLA, AND THE MEMORY OF MY LATE PARENTS

Contents

The Teacher's Place

Carelessly spouting you don't like your teacher
Your teacher may not like you

While learning is the main course of your day
Respect's on the menu too

If spending your time critiquing your teacher
Is your recipe for going over and above

Using that time to enhance your own growth
Leaves little for you to fall in love

A teacher's duty is to educate you
And your purpose there is to learn

What you will need to accomplish in life
Your teacher has already earned

Tolerance and respect are necessities in life
That determines how far you'll get

Someday when you find yourself in charge
You will realize both are assets

Respect the classroom as a teacher's boundary
That you're allowed for a time to cross

An invitation to accept with grace and humility
If misused, is a credit to your loss

(2008)

Basic Training

If you asked someone, "May I...?"
To grant your wish they would

But told when you asked, "Can I...?"
Only you knew if you could

How old were you really
When you learned to say please

And were you taught to cover your mouth
When coughing or if you sneezed

You do say, "Please excuse me!"
If you brush against someone's knee

Or when you've backed into someone
That you really didn't see

When someone opens or holds the door
For you to enter or go through

Do you appreciate the courtesy
By returning a kind "Thank you"?

Were you taught it should be you
Who speak when you enter a room

Or you leave questions of home training
To wonder... and just loom?

Maybe you didn't know there are times you speak
Only when you're spoken to

Or does your mouth have a mind of its own
As if no one matters but you?

Do you ever consider yourself to be
Someone that's very smart

When your tongue stumbles out of bound
With gossip you're dying to impart?

You do realize for every lie you tell
You have to tell one for its cover

And you found after that second lie
You had to come up with yet another

Were you told never to treat others
In a way you wouldn't want to be

That compassion, empathy and respect is what
You show or give without a fee?

And how about speaking up for others
When you see them being mistreated

Making every effort to defuse a fight
That leaves no one defeated?

Don't make life a personal battle
When you are drowning in dos and don'ts

There are times you'll win in life
But there are also times you won't

When asked to do a simple task
You choose to rave and rant

Knowing anything worth getting done
You can before you can't

And what if every little girl and boy
Could learn when just a child

The work they put into a scowling face
Is so much less with a smile?

(2009)

Battling Impressions

You may have first impressions of me
With idle reasons to despise

But judging me by looks alone
Is truly an unfair bias

The habit of labeling by appearance
Putting one in a particular mould

Righteous impressions of someone else
Says more about one's own soul

Shrouded forever under a multitude
Of different faiths, cultures and races

We should be conscious that each and every one
Is worthy of God's good graces

When listening to what a person has to say
Much can be learned from the start

Taking their journey beyond first impressions
Gives a peek inside their heart

(1998)

The Last Goodbye

Coordinating pills and vital sign checks
Following doctor's orders to the letter
Amid beeping monitors and life preserving drips
I tried bargaining with God to make you better

The agony of a moment-to-moment vigil
Anchored firmly in a comfortless chair
Nurses breezed in and out of your room
All you never knew had been there

Hanging around beyond visiting hours
Just to know there was nothing I'd miss
You'd fall asleep and I'd straighten your covers
And on your forehead or hand plant a kiss

I'd watch you struggling day by day
Hoping somehow you'd win your fight
I'd go home, wander around before going to bed
Only to lie awake much of the night

I reveled in the times we had together
Marveling at your age of eighty-nine
It's sobering when statistics suggest you've lived
Your life and maybe part of mine

Your condition was unchanged the day I left
With streaming tears and swollen eyes
Then the call came that you'd gone in the night
Sadly, I'd missed our last goodbye

(2003)

Sierra's Baby Girl Blues

What have I done
With a boy I hardly knew
That promised me the world
Like Mama said he'd do

She had warned many times that Kenny
Was trouble and much too old
Convinced that any girl of fifteen
Is ripe for domination and control

Often told I was like a little woman
Kenny boasted about being a man
Mama says most boys are full of promise
But she's never seen one with a plan

Kenny and I talked about getting married
And how together we'd live our lives
But passion between us got in the way
Before figuring out how we'd survive

I want him to know he's becoming a dad
But I'm afraid if I tell him he'd leave
Everyone is saying, this baby he doesn't want
And one that I surely don't need

He has two children already, I keep hearing
That he hasn't been giving a dime
And he was gone for more than three years
Doing time for some other crime

*****

A neighbor's been hinting about my weight
So I have to be careful what I wear
Mama's gone a lot, and she doesn't know much
About the life that Kenny and I share

Where did I go wrong? What did I miss?
In making this child-to-mom leap
I now see there are so many promises
To this baby I alone can't keep

My hopes…my dreams…and Mama's plans
Are left idle and standing still
An innocent baby is on the way
And its daddy's doing nothing but chill

He's not around to help with decisions
That I'm too young to make for myself
There's no one to rely or depend upon
Except the mercy of my family's help

*****

All the while I thought Mama didn't know
She was well ahead of the game
Convinced that Kenny's my baby's father
She's adamant that he shares the blame

I know she is saddened and disappointed
As she expresses to me life lessons
That sometimes experience is the only teacher
When we shake off advice and don't listen

I trusted Kenny as he professed his love
Saying he would always be around
Now that the baby's already here
He's nowhere in sight to be found

Mama used to talk about other young girls
Saddled...with the baby girl blues
Too young to work, marry or care for themselves
And make decisions like grownups do

That in her day, a baby out of wedlock
Was reason for a girl to hide
Seems today our approach to motherhood
Is done with a sense of pride

My little boy is getting older now
And like a weed he's beginning to grow
But last night someone drove by and shot Kenny
Killing the father he'll never know

(2002)

Deeper Than Skin

As a young boy growing up with Grandma
Not looking like anyone else
My hunger and eagerness for making small talk
Became a sport to entertain myself

Curious stares at my curly, kinky hair
And skin that was lighter than most
I was teased and called the boy in-between
Even a relative of Casper the Ghost

One of four children in our household
With parents one black and one white
Like me, a curly-headed sister but darker
The others blond and extremely light

With Mama and Daddy plagued with their vices
Suddenly our family unit was gone
I, the only boy, went to live with Grandma
As my sisters were shuttled to foster homes

A child's perception of what went wrong
I was told I would never understand
But I saw firsthand Daddy's drowning in booze
And I knew Mama had another man

Grandma would say we had no choosing
In the choices our parents made
To concentrate on whom God wanted me to be
And ignore those trying to denigrate

Constantly reminded how special I was
She'd encourage me just to be myself

To spend my time on being a good boy
And stop worrying about everybody else

Often told if I'd look throughout the family
I'd find all colors of my kin
And the love for me was not black or white
But feelings much deeper than skin

(1976)

Blueprints for Peace

No secrets of the trouble in race relations
Hide the attitudes that feed its defeat
But we cannot continue to saddle our young
With old history they need not repeat

Years of shameful and unjust baggage
In their lives we've managed to smuggle
Our history we want them to build upon
But not as a lifelong struggle

Racial behavior and disgraces of the past
By common threads we're woven and sewn
When blaming, shaming and playing racial games
Ignorance and hate is passed on

While trying to purge hate from racist hearts
Or pry thoughts of evil from the mind
Character screams out from the human blueprint
Building me! Cloaks the spirit over time

Little children are our blueprints for peace
And perfect teachers on how to relate
Sadly, innocence is trapped in a survival setting
And many learn from someone how to hate

Engaging and embracing the diversity of all
Teaches respect for themselves as well as others
Allowing them to live life as God intended
They'll act more like sisters and brothers

(2005)

Beyond Duty

A candid talk and pact with my mother
Of plans for the life I'd lead
Revealing my goal of service to country
Agendas quickly clashed over needs

Beyond the standoff, it was soon apparent
She harbored an avalanche of tears
After endless talks and compromise
My goals finally trumped her fears

On a journey for which I was never prepared
To lose both friends and foe
Promised opportunity and the adventures of travel
From my psyche the excitement flowed

But leaving the comforts of my own home
The silent fears of feeling alone
I never imagined being dropped into a jungle
For a mission that I now own

Finding the selling features of this journey
Presented only lives of the oppressed
My duty became a day-by-day countdown
To leave a country mired in a tangled mess

Completion of duty came not as planned
I had an eagerness to get back home
I am not the same person as when I left
With parts of me forever gone

No longer the hunk that lived next door
Or the boy with the handsome face

Missing an arm, and part of my chin and scalp
My only leg is in a brace

Contributions I left to broken lives
Resurge freely to haunt me still
Of the times there was little to decide
In dismay, it was kill or be killed

The anchors for my ego and pride
Rewarded me with medals and merits
Commendations that will never replace
The fire lost in my fighting spirit

War challenges I thought I'd left behind
I found many of them waiting back home
Returning to embrace the land of the free
Presents a war inside and out that I own

(2005)

A Mirror's Edge

Candid reflections of a mirror's edge
Caught the dance of billowing hips
With a shadow beyond its present hope
Esteem struggled to hold its grip

A pubescent battle for being slighted
When dealt golf-ball-sized breasts
A ghostly voice echoes from the ashes
Cherish! That flat healthy chest

Mirrors take honor in reflecting distress
Of what God has made…no more, no less
Like a hill to climb…or a bridge to cross
Nothing is overcome through shallowness

Who and why am I yearning to see
What God saw no purpose in giving me?
I struggle with whispers…urging silently
I only made you who you need to be

(2007)

Father's Day

Poverty continued to hold its grip
As contentment sprung from Mama's lips
Tomorrow we're told there'd be food to eat
Maybe enough for a special treat

This morning her special letter came
As usual her story is always the same
There are bills to pay along with the rent
Again the money and our feelings are spent

Despite Mama's downer, joy settled in
Dad called, we thought to pick us up again
But this time he wasn't coming for us
Like always he again betrayed our trust

Not been seen around here for days
He appeared for a one-night stay
An evening with Mama, they're a perfect pair
But we knew he'd leave her in despair

He left before we were out of bed
Dishes in the sink meant he'd been fed
Mama left for work on the other side of town
And us with empty promises again let down

(1982)

The Undaunted Host

Family showed up early, unannounced
For a gathering as though it was law
Giving no thought to confirm dinner plans
Or hint of a turkey's time to thaw

A hostess allowed little time to think
How this holiday setting was slanted
She'd stare liberally over the ravenous guests
And how firmly every butt was planted

Feasting with cheer and sighs of thanks
For the privilege to share a stuffed bird
They bowed faithfully in shared prayer
Eagerly closing with the "Amen" word

With clinking and clanking of silverware
Digging in, cheerfully reveling to meet
Giving praise for the delicious meal
And glory to the hostess for the feast

They ate heartily, passing dishes around
Amid the cheerful and raucous laughter
The hostess worked steadily ensuring their joy
Managing time and food like a master

As everyone had been wined and dined
Rambunctious youth fought to entertain
The tolerant host spoke of immense pleasure
To serve family and friends again

As the evening was ending its second phase
Pleasured guests settled in to unwind

The hostess signaled everyone's attention
To reveal what was plaguing her mind

Announcing the cancellation of her yearly feast
Puzzled some, others were kind but unpleased
A tradition of servitude came to its end
As they wistfully packed up to leave

(2005)

Class Action

Before lesson make-ups and extra credit
There were schools lacking sports and any arts
Bad grammar, teachers weren't afraid to correct
And lessons we learned from the start

Few strides were made replacing outdated books
With most severely worn and tattered
Worse yet, our accomplishments were rarely included
Needing to read, it wasn't supposed to matter

Many who fought and died for the right
To peek inside life's treasure chest
Left a legacy of tools to build our dreams
Upon which their laurels rest

There's a need in educating every child
Though much of it we no longer abide
Crippled minds that say who can and who can't
On their backs embittered hearts will ride

To allow a system filled with stumbling blocks
And inequities to deter our goals
Freedom is useless if we still confine
Our mind due to another's poison soul

Education should not be denied or squandered
And dismissed in agony over need
Our children must be inspired to take the reins
Of this proven cornerstone to succeed

(2002)

All Stars Don't Shine

As light rises on the world's confusion
Freedom is stolen and denied
Hate, greed and other intrusions
Leave feelings stretched and tried

God poses among the hovering stars
That sprinkle the midnight sky
To capture all of our behavior scars
With each curious and roving eye

There's never a given time or place
Scars and stars will show or shine
When darkness freely inhabits the heart
It can ravage a trusting mind

Beware of the stars planted among us
Adeptly hiding the darkness they feel
Their glitter and shine knocks us off course
And our human emotions they'll steal

Many will clamor for the spotlight
Bringing behaviors of every kind
A warring thirst and hunger for star power
Only to find all stars don't shine

(2004)

Silent Journey

Drifting into silence
Our conversation would fade
Absent were the claims
Of any progress she'd made

Her mind struggled
In the depths of an abyss
No way was I prepared
For what I'd come to miss

Generations of history
Was being erased
As impatience and agitation
Clouded Mama's face

Her eyes glistened
Like dew on a lawn
She stared as if I
Was no one she'd known

I could see her mind
Ticking like a clock
Trying to speak from a voice
That was seemingly locked

Sensing her frustrations
And feeling like a stranger
On the horizon
Loomed an unsettling danger

She asked about someone
Of whom I'd never heard

I sat graciously, listening
To every foreign word

Emerging from the darkness
Of my own recall
Compared to hers
Mine was trivially small

Speaking frankly though
She'd earned her right to fight
Over times and situations
She tried to shed light

There were no promises
But I was clinging to hope
That I'd summon enough memories
To help me cope

The noise and chatter
As children ran in and out
Suggested they were oblivious
To the tragedy coming about

They treated her behavior
As though it was protocol
While I hung on to every word
No matter how small

Suddenly, after a pensive stare
She asked whose daughter was I
The fleeting smile I flashed
Left tears standing by

Her memory has faded
And there's no one to blame

It's not so far fetched
She'd forgotten my name

I wasn't a friendly face
She'd see everyday
Perhaps my absence
Had gotten in the way

We are both abandoned
And I'm forced to realize
This loss hurts far beyond
My being recognized

Still her mind's demise
Permits a bit of healing
As her affinity with children
Allows a peek at what she's feeling

Her attention and conversation
With a four-year-old boy
Lends a moment to rejoice
As dementia steals our joy

(2000)

The Unlikely Offender

After the Lord's Prayer
And the Pledge of Allegiance
Every morning a silly song would follow
Never thinking of prayer as an offender
Of the assembly of a group of scholars

Daring to make a fuss
Over any religion
Or the reasons that we prayed
To us it was just the beginning of class
And the start of another long day

Beginning today
With prayer and devotion
With some holds little affection
Amid spoken words or meditation
Is a simple request for God's protection

The lack of concern
And little or no respect
Between many teachers and their students
The usual carelessness in parent behavior
Is perhaps why their approach is so prudent

The teacher's mission
In school is to teach
And learning is the child's for being there
Spending all day cooped up with thirty strangers
It's the teacher in need of a prayer

(2001)

A Gathering of Strangers

Like the rumbling of a stampeding herd
Faces masked in fear and worry
In flight is a gathering of strangers
Plagued with every imaginable story
Despite their trials they manage to cling
To a spirit that's uniquely their own
Watching desperately over their family of kin
And trapped with others they've never known

The spell of the eerie moonlight shines
On the silhouette of an exodus for miles
Cloaked in a boundless strength of endurance
Despite being on the run for a while
The charcoal sky lightly sprinkled with stars
Is prime for shielding them in the field
Stragglers idle under the power of its glow
With testaments of unbroken will

Survival has peaked for many as their passion
So cherished belongings they've left behind
More consumed and seasoned with sadness
A sense of peace they're desperate to find
Some seek refuge for a needed rest
Before pushing on to safer grounds
Others are afraid of being beaten or killed
So they trek on to reach the next town

Gripping hunger becomes excess baggage
On a journey that could last for days
Some cling to hope, stretching meager rations
As the weak and feeble die on the way
Their escape is just another upheaval

Of chaos and danger on the move
The spirits and souls are again unduly tested
Of many fleeing their second coup

(2000)

A Cry in the Dark

Approaching home I heard noises coming
From the alley of a back street

As fear in my heart pumped furiously
I wasn't quite sure who I'd meet

The darkened street revealed human frames
And yellow tape wrapped around trees

On the ground lay silent, a contorted figure
And someone bending on their knees

Walking steady and fast, glancing now and then
Over one shoulder, then the other

The voice I heard screaming out in the distance
Was the desperate cry of a mother

Kneeling, weeping and rocking her son
Trying to cradle his head in her lap

To the watchers, he was dead already
But to her…he was taking a nap

Officers requested of those on the scene
The standard query for leads or tips

As usual, no one admitted seeing the shooter
Just the usual assembly of tight lips

The weeping and wailing of family and friends
Made the situation hard to bear

As the body was lifted and carried away
A chilling stillness loomed in the air

(2004)

A Child in Waiting

A child who bullies, pushes and shoves
Is only a child crying out to be loved
A child whose need goes beyond a hint
As my father I'm simply your print

If you're to teach me how to be brave
Teach me first how to behave
You need not reward me for being bold
If I lack character and self-control

With guidance and discipline you should see
The model behavior you want from me
As the parent, if you show me your own
No doubt you'll see mine when I'm grown

My loneliness…has no given time
For excuses when you're never around
And please don't make me feel as I grow
I'm just a seed there was no need to sow

(1999)

Spoiled Fruit

Her wondering silence leaves little trace
But a glimpse of her depression

The indomitable spirit she once embraced
Reveals a deep and painful expression

Her pride of being was a quick-witted mind
Now frail like leaves in the fall

Haughty, arrogant, and insultingly unkind
From life's trappings she's severely mauled

Once a pure and humble heart
Now an old soul mired in turmoil

A loyal spirit that's gone awry
She's like a fruit that's begun to spoil

(2003)

Yesterday's Slave

Happily rescued from the streets
A child's joy I was hoping to find
The caring family that came to my aid
I'm forced to clean up behind

I rise daily, long before the sun
Greeting another day of servitude
Caring for children much older than me
Taking pride in permissive abuse

I've never been able to close my eyes
With the safety and privilege to sleep
Though I've never neglected to do my chores
I lack any contract to feel free

I am not allowed to sit at the table
To enjoy with the family a meal
They, I was told had adopted me
But I'm only a slave…and their deal

The man of the house takes liberties
Far beyond where he should be going
But I can't handle another blinding strike
So it's best his wife not knowing

I've never seen the inside of a school
My learning's not a worthy matter
Never given a stitch of anything to wear
That's not severely worn and tattered

Despite day-to-day back-breaking chores
Silently hiding my aches and pains

Medical care is never available to me
So I dare not whine or complain

The level of comfort I expected to find
Exists nowhere in this home
Despite promised refuge as part of a family
Slave matters are all that I own

(2010)

Christmas Eve

Christmas Eve meant window washing
And decorating with snow from a can
An exhausting feat just to welcome in
An overweight, bearded white man

A long-leaf pine dragged from the forest
Its branches unevenly laced
We'd carefully drape and balance skimpy lights
Trying to fill each hollow space

Cookies and candies were in abundance
Despite threats of damage to our teeth
The aroma of fruits courted our senses
But none filled the void of sweet treats

Jittery anticipation was running rampant
When told Santa was on his way
The pressures of an overweight, bearded white man
Promising to land on our roof in a sleigh

We'd scurry off to bed in half-hearted fear
Of ashes being thrown in our eyes
With visions of Santa getting stuck in the chimney
All because of his opulent size

Santa's look or who he was never mattered
As long as he delivered our toys
Nearly smothering while pretending to sleep
In a struggle as model girls and boys

He'd leave a doll with pasty skin
Resembling no one on our family tree

Whose only movement was a gentle noise
As her eyes rolled up to see

Among the presents left under the tree
Games and books were never spared
The clothing as long as they were our own
We never minded a bike being shared

(2010)

A Sea of Women

The wandering of a man's spirit
Aimlessly among those he discards
All those lonely, big-hearted women
With no regrets or regards
Before I could ever utter a word
Or attempt to have my say
My voice was drowned by some louder mouth
Determined to get in my way

Your invitation signaled a warning
Arrive early to secure my place
Discovering this sea of desperate women
Is a fruitless and dreaded race
What other route of appreciation
Would show that I'd been here
It was useless to yell, or shout out your name
Among wenches in screaming tears

From an audience that's loose and foolish
You've earned the ranking of a king
Before panting hearts and raining eyes
Yet promising not a thing
Caught up in this groupie spell
And passionate gyrations on stage
Salivating...screaming women from every town
Too many, so advanced in age

But what is this shallow fantasy
With you, yet seen or known
Watching this sea of desperate women
Feed an ego so overblown
Competing for such fleeting affections

Known to plant hearts in early graves
I'd rather move on and shade new ground
Than remain your anonymous slave

(2009)

Confessions of a Mother

She was ushered in, and I knew nothing
But to scramble for lessons in motherhood
No instructions came packed with this bundle
And most of what I'd read was no good

This angel before me as she was seen
The most beautiful baby ever born
With her I fell intensely in love
And I shouldn't be blamed for feeling torn

God bestowed good health upon this child
Along with relatively good looks
Further blessing me with instincts and common sense
Not to trust everything in a book

Many times I would just sit and stare
At the silence and her faintest moves
In a struggling resistance to close my eyes
As she redesigned the sleep I'd lose

Watching her grow and manage daily life
Dance and other activities that matter
It's refreshing to watch her interacting with others
Much I'd dismiss as mindless chatter

Now that she's grown up into her own
I am filled with a mother's pride
That allows me to sit back and enjoy the trip
As she buckles up for life's bumpy ride

(2005)

Spirits in the Woods

Every sweltering second Sunday in August
Our church held its annual big meeting
Members and their families showed up in the masses
All anticipating a day of good eating

After a speedy service the congregation scattered
With the preacher shaking a hand or two
As many members assembled for idle chatter
For him the time to feast was overdue

Tables were draped with crisp white linens
Topped with dishes abundantly spread
A variety of vegetable, salad and meat platters
Festive desserts and an assortment of breads

To embrace and combat the intrusive heat
There were plenty of thirst quenching goods
While wives in the pews were shouting amen to a sermon
A few husbands snuck off to the woods

The presence of men seen on church grounds
Were many that had been missing inside
To the preacher it never seemed a worthy matter
He'd dismissed their absence in stride

As sisters graciously filled the preacher's plate
Certain dishes seemed to nudge his stroll
Wiping his brow he'd direct liberal helpings
To feed a girth already on a roll

Two disheveled old men journeyed up the trail
Suspicious though steady on their feet

Dewey eyed and heavily beaded in sweat
Smelling of spirits drawn out by the heat

On a winding path through a thicket of pines
Under a tangled swell of bullet vines
Prayer and faith finally met the competition
Of beer, White Lightning and wine

One by one they ambled out of the woods
Merging and mingling with spiritual rebirth
Many loitered near their holy but chilly wives
After a fun day in their sinful mirth

(2002)

Gun of a Son

A father with a son attempts to mould
As a man to be brave and bold

Confusing free spirit with a loosened grip
Sometimes there's a needed scold

A child with little interest in playing sports
That most boys would find a charm

Feeds his fantasy in the lure of other games
Harming much more than legs and arms

Given his own gun and shooting stuff
Like a man he seems rough and tough

A weapon he's taught to shoot with ease
When he's not quite mature enough

Neglecting to teach the value of life
Before placing a gun in his hand

All the expert shooting skills in the world
Won't validate him as a man

It's important that a child should not be rushed
In harm's way with little or no defense

As the body may look and feel matured
Its mind is unequal in common sense

(2003)

Linking Scars

Their scars are not from the cracks of whips
Or a lashing from the white man
But gifts of bullets and dull machetes
Cold merits, doled from black hands

Families move hurriedly in exodus
Men and boys, as they flee are mowed down
Mothers with plagued and sickened babies in tow
Seek refuge on safer grounds

As they quietly ponder their endless plight
In a land that's so richly revered
A penance of the freedom the world celebrates
They're crowned in a shackle of fears

The young suffer scars far beyond healing
And there's guilt for the dignity they lack
At the hands of their own, they're being burned
Where sanity hardly makes its way back

(2002)

Tears beneath Pain

The strength of a man is a common belief
That grief should never be shown
As all hearts ache, they also weaken
And the broken is just as prone

A mournful heart summons enough breath
To release its feelings without fear
In an uncontrollable private weep
Or the times you only shed a tear

There comes a time we all may need
The comfort of another's hand
As the hurt from grief and sorrow hide
The tears beneath our pain

There is a need to abandon the notion
That a man's not supposed to cry
As your soul, like mine, trembles inside
Without feelings or emotion it will die

(2001)

The Neighbor's Table

In the dead of night
While settled in bed
Out of silence
Came a jarring alarm
Fluttering and cackling
Their anxious cry
Signaled something's
In the henhouse doing harm

The pulse of a neighbor
That crept in the night
Prompted a stillness
And a change in mood
In the early hours
During the morning feed
There was one less
Chick in the brood

Except a few feathers
Left in the scuffle
Finding the thief
We just weren't able
Then Mama's impromptu
Visit at dinnertime
Found a plump hen
On the neighbor's table

Man or weasel
The thief had no name
As suspicions
Were allowed to linger
Until the next-door neighbor

Choked with guilt
At her husband
She pointed the finger

(2005)

Distant Voices

I. Anticipation

My feet... unsteady on this shaky ground
As a splint holds my leg in place
Amid the sea of distant stares and voices
There are questions clouding every face

Our needs have long been ignored
Too many years of enduring hell
A dare and grave risk when asking why
Was an invitation to check out the jail

A faint voice echoes in the distance
Of life somewhere in the rubble
When cries die into an eerie silence
Someone's exhausted in their trouble

With stained gauze wrapped around my head
A bruised foot no longer fitting my shoe
A broken ankle that's stolen my gait
Abandonment is slowly becoming truth

Where is the man that sat in the Palace?
And his Cronies, where have they all gone
Have they, as the rogues and thieves before
Escaped to their vacation homes?

A whiff of stench cruises the balmy air
From the ballooning bodies of two men
Between them a sign of their noontime frolic
There lay a half bottle of gin

Again, a faint voice is calling out
There's still life somewhere in the distance
Men dig, lifting debris with bare hands
Ignoring a desperate need for assistance

II. Famine

Chaos is taking an ugly hold
On many, becoming desperate for food
Tents are popping up in mass clusters
For many stuck in hopeless moods

Hunger is scratching at every back
Food and water is a pressing need
With perishing flesh scattered about
A stubborn stench crushes desires to eat

Our suffering is fast approaching day three
While supplies still wait at the port
The need for food and medical care mounts
Amid symptoms of dwindling support

Shot by police two men accused of looting
Clutch bags of food as they flee
While one escapes the other lay dead
As onlookers learn theft has a fee

With loyalty, debate hangs over the scene
Where it's obvious everyone needs a meal
There's no official or clear-cut policy
Or any order of shoot to kill

III. The Phantom of Youth

As sadness grips the faces of babes
You want to kiss away their tears

Many destined to join their fellow orphans
With a future of uncertain fears

Facing a life like none they've known
Hearing raps and taps in the rubble
Perhaps someone dear is still entombed
But can't be freed from their trouble

Only innocence perished in their school
With a few to be found alive
Watching classmates heaped on the bed of a truck
And hauled off to the countryside

A girl lay with twilight in her eyes
As her mother waits anxiously at her side
Her tear-streaked face is the only sign
She knows her child has already died

A stolen or borrowed crypt to rest
Or perhaps just one to share
But who should worry where remains are laid
In this shower of horror and despair

IV. The Exodus

As prison doors flung open, the unsavory fled
Leaving a stable of empty cells
They've freely filtered into the crowd
But who cares? And who is there to tell?

A carnival of people parading in
A brief movement shifting their feet
Another rumble they feel is a threat away
So they strike out racing through the streets

Anxiously, boarding buses and ferries
Many are pushed aboard in despair
With growing fears of another quake
They seek destinations to anywhere

A young mother reluctantly boards a bus
Her two children perished in the quake
When asked if they had the courtesy of burial
She whispered they'd been thrown away

At the port, silence looms over cracked runways
As vehicles stop struggling to move around
Food and water becomes an infinite hostage
As tires are no match for broken ground

V. Is This the Season

Lord, your house is unstable this morning
So we worship you across the street
Keep your eyes hovering over us
And steady the ground beneath our feet

Engulfed and trapped in the sweltering heat
Just baked by the sun above
There's still no food or water in sight
But we hang on, in faith of your love

As we gather this morning for prayer and worship
If I might ask, God…is this the season
To impose your will…we only ask
Though we have no right to your reasons

Innocence cloaks the tiniest souls
Their eyes hollow with wonder and despair
The elders look with certainty and wisdom
Forgiving the missing care

Many remain faithfully by the side
Of family members that are obviously dead
Nursing their own wounds and broken limbs
Or minor cuts and bruises to the head

Who is this strange doctor man?
That's kneeling to hear my cry
He talks, and explains as he takes my hand
With efforts to assure I'll get by

He doesn't know, I've been told before
That help is on the way—for me
While lying with child in this spot for a while
And this happens to be day three

Daily, supplies still wait in abundance
For the people, but can't get across
We're patient, but help needs to arrive
To curb this unnecessary loss

Bodies are randomly strewn about
As a rebellious stench hangs around
A swipe of anything with a fragrant hint
Is welcome but nowhere to be found

VI. A Child's Cry

I am now a restavek
A few pennies for my head
Welcoming destiny to anywhere
My family…everyone I know is dead

Enslaved! Now by Mother Nature
As orphans belonging no place
We're at risk of being sold off by kin
Or abandoned to end up as slaves

In this grueling test of life
We can't play with smiling faces
You wonder if my resilience is waning
Nothing's left in this unholy place

Our minds and bodies need repair
On our soul there's been a raid
A wound too big for another quick fix
God, only you can aid

Know that you have shaken us
You have too, awakened us
We are broken in so many places
A needed cleanse shall redeem us

The heavens! For those taken from us
Out of misery, but not your love
We're all in peril and needing hope
To survive as you keep watch above

(2010)

A Chat with Ms. Anne

A stranger's judgment heaped upon me
Is fair if not gossiped or guessed
Sharing what's inhabited all of my life
Is a spirit and soul I know best

My life is under temporal surveillance
No matter where I go or what I do
You can't convince me that I'm paranoid
So here's my heads-up to you

I have neither the will, desire, nor the time
To spend debating life with you
Time's too valuable, and I'm too absorbed
In the spiritual things I do

Surely, you must have noticed by now
Issues aren't just black and white
Your future here, along with mine
Is beginning not to look so bright

Life, no matter how we've known it
Is under radical change as you've seen
It's no longer your determined world
Gray matters hover in between

It's fair to say, maybe some injustice
At most feet are unfairly laid
And if it gives you reason to continue fearing me
Of you…I'm equally afraid

Your focus on me is in overdrive
With efforts to keep me down
It's flooding, be careful you don't soon drown
In your delusions of black and brown

(2003)

Just One Look

Easily impressed as a little girl
Learning from my peers back talk
I couldn't have been much more than four
When shown the path I'd walk

If something was done or said out of place
From Mama we'd get the look
"Change your behavior" blanketed her face
And just that one look it took

She'd make promises to do her best
In providing whatever we'd need
With appeasement in a face of silence
Or a voice that came without a plea

Adept at having the last word
With Mama we knew what to expect
The mood of growing up in our household
From us all she demanded respect

In every home she thought regulation
Was the wisdom in a parent's point of view
Acutely aware of what we could and couldn't do
Headlining her rules was curfew

To her, discipline and unconditional love
Were mandates in raising a child
And her role as parent was to stay in charge
To ensure we didn't run wild

(2001)

Mr. Prince's Field

At times we'd raid Mr. Prince's field
In search of full ripe melons
We'd gorge until our bellies popped
Gaining reputations as felons

A harvest he could have easily sold
Was dispersed throughout the neighborhood
No one had a bigger heart than Mr. Prince
Who insisted helping anyone he could

Friday evenings he'd arrive to tend his crops
His old mule and a plough behind
Never once complaining of marauding vandals
Or the pillage of any crops he'd find

Plowing his field until dusk had fallen
He was never seen leaving for home
Uncommonly still one Saturday at sunrise
His old mule stood quietly alone

As though bowed in a manner of prayer
Amid stillness and a sign of dread
There was no reason to think of cause for alarm
Or any tragedy that lay ahead

With creeping wonder of what happened in the night
We moved with eerie silence to inspect
Mr. Prince it seemed had been dragged to his death
With a rope stressed around his neck

Suddenly in the distance a long black hearse
Rocked and rolled across the newly plowed field

Though the morning had emerged bright and sunny
It was crowned with a dark eerie feel

In the wake of a chilling meltdown of guilt
With us, and throughout the neighborhood
Obedience quickly surged in our behavior
To honor Mr. Prince as we should

Rumors spread of a man frequently seen
Standing idly at the bottom of the hill
Some swore that it could only be Mr. Prince
On guard of his long abandoned field

Passing his home on our way to school
Was when we feared his presence the most
Keeping a hand on our actions from his grave
Scared us straight by rumors of his ghost

(1965)

Family Antiques

The precious antiques of Eden Manor
Are not vases or pictures on a wall
Though many are cracked, some even broken
Others leisurely parade the halls

The antics of the manor's most social pair
Bud and Anna as they are known
Hints a whisper of romance in their actions
Amid faculties that seems a bit blown

Anna enters, sporting a rose in her hair
Fragile and weathered from a lack of care
But in Bud's presence she sparks a glow
Prying at him to notice she's there

For a while he's coy, in his childish spirit
And worn-out trousers that don't fit
Then blankets her in his wild-eyed glee
A raw innocence and play she permits

She smiles and prances, prompting his attention
A humor in each other they find
Curious noises of housemates fill the halls
That neither seem to notice or mind

To any worker, visitor or passer-by
Bud's hand he'd proudly extend
With some reluctant to shake or even touch
Signals wonder as to where they'd been

War veteran, Miss Sally mumbles a profane past
Setting rules without house consent

It's Sunday morning and she's dressed in her finest
Boarding a bus for church to repent

From New York hails the queen, Miss Mary
Speaking proudly of her precious Prince
A spiffy old gal and resident for six years
Hasn't seen this beloved son since

Monday night she livens up activity hall
With those amble enough to get around
A few quarters securely tucked in their pockets
To fund a number of bingo rounds

A young newcomer known as Crazy Mable
Quickly established herself on manor grounds
A stroke victim whose gait has been stolen
She's graced with wearing the bingo crown

While many residents sit slumped in wheelchairs
Some hardly ever leaving their rooms
Though quietly hushed in their private worlds
Fun exists amongst the gloom and doom

(2004)

The Blank Canvas

I've arrived!
Now, I didn't bring much
But I'm here and ready to roll
Though a little noisy and whiney at times
I'm fine with you in control

A seed!
You'd never sow and abandon
To germinate and grow wildly on its own
So think of my growth like the spread of a vine
You nurture before it's overgrown

Yeah!
You may think I'm precious and cute
And someone to behold and cherish
Unless some firmness and discipline is applied
Respect for you will undoubtedly perish

I'm a child!
Spare me your life details
And the troubles with which you collide
Since my life should be free and simple
From me much of yours you should hide

Guide me!
So that I may grow
With the knowledge only you should teach
Realize, it's not enough just giving me life
So your contract as a parent isn't breached

Literally!
I could be a portrait

Of your fine yield and precision
But careful your character doesn't lose its footing
And my future is wrecked in the collision

You could!
Just think of me as a blank canvas
Upon which my character is drawn
And if you're carefully guiding your strokes
Your artistry will be proudly shown

(2003)

Hollow Hell

Little children using words
They don't know and can't spell
Patience waits outside
The gates of hollow hell

Allow them to lie
They'll learn to cheat well
As the freedom door beckons
Entrance to hollow hell

Permit a curt and sassy tongue
And debating authority to swell
Inevitably the freedom door
Will swing open to hollow hell

Allowing youth to do as they please
When their attitude begins to smell:
Caution! The door to that newfound freedom
Is wide open to hollow hell

Justifying a parent's lack of control
Peddling free expression for sale
Privilege is out of the stall and running
Through the gates of hollow hell

Cloaked and enamored in gripping sin
Of behavior they hide, and can't tell
For this wretched soul, accommodations await
Residence in hollow hell

As a parent shrouded in a burden of guilt
And feeling you've somehow failed
Only God's reign on this wandering spirit
Steers them out of hollow hell

(2001)

Juvenility

Values and morals
Are by parents taught
In hopes by their young
Their advice is sought

We preach to them
Because they simply don't know
That the words of an elder
Is their tonic to grow

Few heed our words
And admonishments
Much they already know
Lacks common sense

Sometimes with trouble
Their lives are fraught
As they often disappoint
And leave us distraught

But we fail to remember
Our own recklessness
Of flaws and foolishness
We'd never confess

Carelessness is just
A condition of the young
If we remember and admit
Our youth of not so long

(2002)

Juvenescence

Often between parents and their youth
Ideas will inevitably collide
There's a need for sufficient space and trust
As teens, they too have their pride

Children will say things randomly
Just to arouse or evoke a reaction
The difference in your child's behavior and yours
Is probably no more than a fraction

Talk openly with them as often as possible
Allowing time for free expression
Listen closely though to what's being said
There's often a slip-up confession

Be careful in giving too much praise
It's a green light to becoming too cocky
Mind when and where to lodge a critique
Dueling egos can get a little rocky

Allow their spirits to be open and free
Cautioning what should and shouldn't be
They'll learn to experience life in their own realm
With little dependence on you and me

(2001)

Godsends

God sends a friend to run errands
When we're shut in, or sick in bed

God sends a friend to ensure peace and quiet
Just to sooth an aching head

God sends a friend to be the voice
When unable to speak for one's self

God sends a friend that believes in us
When there's support from no one else

God sends a friend with an honest opinion
But knows when to bite their tongue

God sends a friend to applaud when we're right
But scold us when we're wrong

God sends a friend who will offer compromise
Whenever our ideas clash

God sends a friend who will pay for a meal
If we happen to be short on cash

God sends many friends that will come and go
And some will remain 'til the end

Just hope God gives the wisdom to recognize
The true ones as Godsends

(2002)

Heaven Bound

Young soldiers lurk to create fear
Their minds duly poisoned and bribed
Lacking humility beyond compare
Stirring vicious feuds between tribes

Babies with glossed eyes knock at death's door
Seeking the cloak of angel wings
As plagues of sickness sprinkle the fertile floors
Where warlords reign as kings

The haunting burdens little children bear
To surrender their virtue untouched
An abuse of their innocence chances disgrace
And denies them peace as such

Caretakers fleeing with meager belongings
In tattered frocks without stitches
Above this haven of precious earth
Exiled from their birthright of riches

This larceny of life from the young and old
With closed eyes we pretend not to see
An existence of freedom that has undersold
The pitied souls we fail to keep

Dust and ashes, they must lie in heaven
For dying and not knowing why
Hell must be reserved for those of us
Who willfully turns a blinding eye

(2002)

Stream of Fear

Gushing water
Smashed against my head
Like a toad scrambling
To reach the ground

Swept away
In a current so strong
I thought within minutes
I'd drown

I shook in terror
From head to toe
In a furious float
Downstream

Coming to rest
Under a marshy brush
So dense I could
Hardly be seen

I called out
In a trembling voice
Hoping to hear someone
Shouting back

I lay there thinking
For a while, perhaps
They'd find
And follow my tracks

Lodged beneath
A pile of stubborn brush

And unable to
Free myself

Writhing and praying
A twig suddenly snapped
As my weakened body
Released itself

(2001)

Oh, Nurse!

A little mishap
Have you down and out
And the pain following
Needles…you say
Keep the pompous attitude
And will that you've got
You'll soon be up
And on your way

Your nurse enters
With a prescription dose
Carrying a tray
With a pill or two: She…is not
What the doctor ordered
To ease the pain
You're going through

Obey the doctor
Take what he prescribes
To ease your aches and pains
You'll be up and about
In no time at all
Doing whatever it is…
You do again

(2003)

The Harbor

There are few people in my daily life
Other than those needing my help

Often demanding long and tedious hours
Leaving little time for myself

To feed the hungry showing up at our door
In need of a meal to eat

Or trying to house those seeking shelter
Who've been forced onto the street

Welcoming a battered wife who fled her home
To escape her husband's hell

Who's trying to protect and convince her child
It was time for daddy's farewell

Homeless, hungry or just beaten down
Nearly all are unemployed

The harbor has long been their only refuge
And relief, but few are overjoyed

These women are all in desperation
And in some way need to be served

With nowhere to go, and no one to turn to
They're infused with attitude and nerve

(1998)

Commandos

Close your eyes, commando…and see if you can feel…

The bond of an infant's coziness
Against the warmth of its mother's breasts
Or do you care that it chokes and gurgles
On rice pabulum it's trying to ingest

Close your eyes, commando…and see if you can feel…

The marriage between a little boy and his toy
As he frolics and romps in the sand
Or that you've stolen the peak of his innocence
By placing a gun in his hand

Close your eyes, commando…and see if you can feel…

The maturation of demure little girls
Robbed of painted faces and nails
That you've forced into early motherhood
Their heads laden with baskets and pails

Close your eyes, commando…and see if you can feel…

A mother's cry to provide her home
With sparse utensils and tools
Or that she's too poor to provide her child
With the basic needs for school

As you close your eyes, commando…surely, you must feel…

An ounce of compassion in your heart
For those whose humanity you steal
Or has the malignancy that's coursing your veins
Eaten any empathy you should feel?

(2003)

The Sideshow

Amid the hustle and bustle on a rushing train
The entertainment's a daily side show
Witnessing riders packed shoulder to shoulder
I search desperately for a face I know

Every corner I look some pervert is nestled
With signs of a mind that's bent
In silence one makes a gesture of lewdness
As his eyes flaunts a haunting intent

Uneasily I'm trying to avoid the flirting
Of another who is determined to tease
Impatiently awaiting the train's next stop
And its door to swing open for my release

I see a wandering hand touching a woman's knee
As she threateningly shoves it away
The nervy jerk attempts to try it again
And a slap's plastered across his face

As the train pulls in, riders rush the door
Frantically highlighting the city's urban breed
Scurrying and scattering as the doors flung open
Once again from this circus I am freed

(2004)

Wild Heat

Gus McGraw sank into his darkest days
At the untimely death of his wife
Daughter Emily is presenting new challenges
In managing a teenager's life

Missed opportunities in discussing her needs
Left a void with no one to fill
For a daughter who's a little grown at sixteen
A parent's care is needed still

With her mother, Emily would sit and discuss
Her becoming sixteen in the fall
Until that day there was no need to think
Any boy would be coming to call

Anxious to test her impending freedom
Paint and polish met face and nails
At the perfect age to pique a boy's interest
She sets out to pursue them as well

An invitation to a brazen young friend
Though risky she's willing to gamble
Her father's trust she thinks she has earned
And any objections she's prepared to handle

With McGraw away at work for the day
She's at ease to let her hair down
While in the kitchen whipping up a snack
Outside, roared a familiar sound

An impromptu return by Old McGraw
In a panic the boy scrambled to hide

Raucously stumbling as he broke and ran
With a cable cord breaking his stride

McGraw, entering with his resounding stomp
Sniffed upon an unexpected find
A strong and unfamiliar brutish scent
Of cheap cologne had been left behind

Civil silence loomed over the room
Though suspicion seemed to cloud the air
Now was not the time for a confrontation
But he knew someone had been there

*****

In church, Emily sits in beads and lace
With her father seated at her side
Stealing glances at his scruffy old face
Clutching thoughts she's trying to hide

Her voice in a tremble, soft and slow
She speaks of a boy for him to meet
He tells her quietly she's a beautiful girl
And soon enough boys will be at her feet

Under a breath of carefully managed words
Whispering she's listened, obeyed and waited
She no longer enjoyed following around
One so senile, testy and outdated

Staring her down, he chides her defiance
Pleading an obedience request
Sighing disappointedly, her face in disgust
She struggles in a silent protest

Determined to introduce this young man
Hopes are dashed as she refrains
But having known each other for so many years
Continued hiding is causing her pain

As the day wore on they headed home
Riding for miles in obvious strain
Suddenly he inquired of the young man's name
Eagerly she blurted out, "Kane"

*****

In the sweltering heat, Kane shuffled the back road
Anxious to meet Emily at her place
His heart thumping and his passions abounding
For just another glimpse of her face

All proper and polished from head to toe
Flashing a coy and boyish smile
He's only aiming to impress the old man
Though he's aware of his limited style

As Kane stood rapping with anxious eyes
Through a cracked door old McGraw peered
Opening the door quickly catching the boy by surprise
As he uttered Emily's name in choking fear

Kane collects himself and in clearer words
Asks again in a tone of demand
Sure to see Emily as he had planned to do
But saw he'd angered the old man

McGraw shouted, as he was known to do
For him to leave before he get riled
Kane slowly nodded with reluctance to go
The old man was cramping his style

Backing away silently as the door closed
He pondered the old man's request
Thinking of ways to win the old goat
For he knew nothing was said in jest

His only goal is to be with Emily
To ensure her unfettered love
But to see her as he'd planned to do
The old man they must get rid of

*****

As night met darkness and still all around
Kane was in full control of his plan
Looming under Emily's window without a sound
Trying desperately to avoid the old man

Much of the night passed without a move
But a stray thought pricked his mind
This plan with Emily she must approve
Creeping silently to her might be unkind

He tossed a pebble that missed her window
Then another that hit the pane
Alerted by the noise she quickly appeared
Raising the window in a grunting strain

In a whisper she inquired of his presence
As she had no knowledge of his plan
Secretly he had arranged their escape
And to hell with pleasing her old man

Now, Emily in her maturing right
Wasn't known for too much aggression
But it's evident in her latest behavior
She is fed up with her father's oppression

She raised her eyes in an upward glance
In a plea of forgiveness from above
With Kane, she was finally convinced
Their escape was her only chance for love

Anxiously thrashing through a cluttered chest
In search of a meager cash reserve
With a vision of them as bride and groom
Fled her room with impudent nerve

Idling quietly at the end of the porch
And whispering in a pensive tone
She was now feeling a surge of abandon
By leaving her old man alone

Pondering with great uncertainty
As Kane stared deep into her face
He professed the love she'd waited to hear
Blanketing her in a smoldering embrace

Taking her hand they started to leave
When they saw in the distance a shadow
From behind the house stepped grim old McGraw
But his presence showed little matter

Emily approached him boldly as he stared
With a steely glare in his eyes
Knowing in his heart that her leaving this way
She'd be permanently out of his life

(1983)

Graffiti

We must teach our children not to destroy
What they had no hand in building
While learning to respect what belong to others
Their conduct we must stop shielding

So often we dismiss their bad behavior
To be nothing more than childish pranks
But when they're allowed to wreck and ruin
Their destruction just grows in rank

Graffiti's not art, and is usually evident
With toddlers in their early expression
When parental guidance and teaching's at hand
It often stifles any further progression

But toddler behavior is not for juveniles
Who by now should know right from wrong
When defacing and scarring what belong to others
There should be no cradle-songs

(2002)

Burdens and Blessings

With grace and unconditional love
Stirring the spirit within our souls
God clears the hurdles in our path
As burdens and blessings unfold

As blessings are heaped upon us
We must keep the faith to know
In our daily tasks if there's a burden
It too will help us grow

With every ounce of toil and strife
God is there for our every need
To grant our daily lease on life
And bless us with Godspeed

He keeps watch over each of us
Seeing the depths of our weary souls
He is the core of our infinite being
Capturing all of our stories untold

Confused by what is confronting us
Just trust that God knows best
Even when life appears to be a burden
We're still by him being blessed

(2016)

God's Moral Creed

As the days fade upon our world's existence
It's mired in shameless disguise
Hate and discord rises around the world
In full view of God's eyes

Restlessness ravages the belly of man
With a thirst and savagery to kill
Courting the young, the naïve and uninformed
As the spill of their blood covers the bill

Many engage war under claims of Religion
With a misguided view of God's desire
Others embrace it for the sake of power
While the manipulation of life goes awry

Our earth is cleansed with timely discretion
Without any needed help from man
Any cleansing should be of our own hearts
And not to interfere with God's plan

Hate and war games will go on forever
Unless we cleanse our hearts of greed
Do we continue killing the soul of our existence
Or seek the spirit of God's Moral Creed?

(2004)

A Rainy Day

For weeks lavender insisted
Spraying the balmy air

Fusing itself with allergies
Urging a doctor's care

In comes a shower of rain
As a rainbow arcs the sky

Plants and trees begin to rejoice
As birds and bees fly by

On the stub of a pillared trunk
New shoots and buds peek out

An invitation to the spring's first rain
Replied with fresh new sprouts

Early flowers in the spring
Fumes a breezy and freshened air

Through the joyous sunshine
Darts bluebirds in a pair

(2001)

Cheers and Leers

Clumsily posing in frills and fluff
High heels, makeup and big hair
In the spotlight, Mom nervously cheers
All at the expense of my care

Forced to grow up at a tender age
And it's happening right under her nose
Like a baby, I'm barely out of diapers
Before lurking perverts I'm exposed

Hair swept up in beehives and pompadours
Instead of braids or Shirley Temple curls
Alluring dress and behavior in a manner
Too inappropriate for little girls

At age six with a flipper in my mouth
Covering missing teeth for pageant glam
When part of growing up is losing my teeth
As a six-year-old, that's who I am

For the first time, I'm riding my bike
And doing it without a third wheel
Imagine sashaying in a pageant parade
Wearing one-and-a-half-inch heels

I could be out playing with dolls
Or some other appropriate toy
Here I am dolled up, parading on stage
Before twisted men and young boys

Family is here to cheer me on
But others showed up to check me out
What better venue or family setting
Than a child exhibit for pedo-scouts

(2009)

God's Looking In

Seeing the heartache
And pain of us all
Every tear we shed
He sees it fall
He knows every thought
That enters our head
And hears every voice
And what's being said
He sees the behavior
Of everyone
And knows every right
And wrong we've done
He knows every problem
That plagues our mind
And offers the comfort
We seek to find
He knows when we're
At the end of our rope
With trust in him
He dispenses hope
Looking in, he sees
The depth of our soul
He knows that we are
All less than whole
And with that perfection
We do not possess
God still deserves
No less than our best

(2005)

My Soul Emptied

A journey into my burdened soul
Encountered forces I am ashamed to tell
Finding no peace in this punishment
Confession's my only freedom in this hell

A tepid suffering in its emptiness
As I search the emotions in my soul
Bearing their wrath is bittersweet
As my childhood collectively unfolds

Barely six years old at a science fair
Navigating my way through warning signs
Had two small trucks from someone's display
Set the course for my future crown?

Removing them went without a hitch
Until a little bird fell from a tree
With the librarian seated at the front of the room
I locked eyes, as he pretended not to see

At nine, lifting cash from the purses and pockets
Of those gracing my family tree
There was never an attempt from any of them
To chastise or even challenge me

At twelve, I took a calculator from a friend
Whom I thought had money to burn
I told Mama the teacher had given them out
As tools that we needed to learn

A lofty arrogance at age fifteen
Prompted me to sell drugs to my friends

Expelled and banned from attending school
For activities that would never end

In the park one evening, I demanded money
From an old man walking with his wife
With a knife in my hand, as they pleaded with me
My soul emptied...I took his life

I sit between these cold empty walls
Having flashes of the librarian's face
Wondering, had he made me return the trucks
Would my life be sentenced in disgrace?

(2007)

Rising Tide

Seasoned love with awakening blows
So little a woman will confide or show
Often her spirit's weak, humble and frail
And hampered blindly within a man's hell

Teetering on a rising tide of contempt
Knowing her limbs are never exempt
Her soul is restless, awaiting his wrath
And what lies in the ruins of its aftermath

To her, passion, romance and all of his games
Are mere images of happiness hidden in shame
The trouble beneath what's accepted as truth
Is a destiny stalled in shades of blue

A mind that's adrift over the past
Held hostage by first encounters…and last
A life that's more in touch with illusions
Leaves a heart ravaged with growing confusion

(2002)

The Beacon

A beaming light
Above my bed
A down pillow
Thrust over my head

Six feet away
The beacon steals
A seat firmly atop
Of the window sill

It seems to follow me
Edging like a spy
But there's no face
To affix any eye

Snuggling silently
In my body's heat
Sweat popping from even
The bottom of my feet

The light disappears
And there's nothing there
As strangeness happens
My room's now bare

A scene of nothingness
A surreal bet
To explain the light's
Existence yet

It's been robbed…
This place of rest

Now stands abandoned
By its fleeting guests

But more elusive
Than anything I've known
A life…The beacon, I guess
Had one of its own

(2006)

The Hapless Soul

Your impromptu visit this morning
Caught me inside peeking out
It's not wise to show up unannounced
When my mind is running about

You may have trouble finding me
With so many places to hide
Don't always look for me in the back
Sometimes I'm sitting on the side

Please! When you arrive, don't just peek in
Come in so we can get acquainted
Don't worry about what you've heard of me
God knows…we're all a bit tainted

If you come when I'm feeling low
While hapless thoughts pry my brain
And if you hurry, you may help banish
Shedding tears from a scourge of pain

A time that's very dark in my soul
I'm not feeling today as I should
Please! Please! Come and rescue me
I'd save myself if I could

(2010)

The Splendor of Spring

When the weather heats up
Birds return to sing

Butterflies are freely
Unfolding their wings

On bone-dried trees
That suffered severe drought

New buds and branches
Have begun to sprout

Fragrant blossoms are beckoning
All species of bees

To feast on the sweetness
In the flowers and trees

Birds set up housekeeping
With twigs and vines

Nesting and singing melodies
In the brush they've entwined

Things that creep and crawl
Are scampering everywhere

On this landscape of nature
They've all come to share

(2004)

The Trapdoor

Like a caged animal
Making a quick dash
Lashing out at seeming pray

A worker ant
Hauling food to its mound
Scrambles to get away

Like a darting bird
Flying into a wall
Recovering from its own knockout

A bed of seeds
Well past germination
Once watered begins to sprout

I'm now free
Of domination and control
Which I was never able to say

This trapdoor
Is suddenly unlatched
What freedom! I've found my way

(2003)

Excess Baggage

Lost within a cosmetic revolution
There's a longing for beauty that tries
To wage its war with Mother Nature
For the pleasure of another's eyes

Many sew or glue weaves on their head
To create the illusion of more hair
And some will bleach deeply pigmented skin
To acquire a look that's more fair

Some burn skin that's lacking in color
While embracing its fleeting appeal
A shimmer not lasting beyond its glow
Before its cosmetics start to peel

Often pinching a nose for narrowness
Or shaving the bridge to rid a hump
Many go for fillers to gain fuller lips
As others freak at the sight of facial bumps

The rash will insert silicone in their breasts
To inflate and push beyond their peak
Later discovering the insertion technique
Is flawed and causing them to leak

Many risk the danger of sucking fat
From hips and thighs to make thinner
Cosmetic procedures often lie within reason
If having the ears cropped or pinned

A swinging desire to enhance mini parts
For a night of unbridled fun

Is like a car that's been idle many years
Pumped with fuel and expected to run

Relying on surgeons and Botox to erase
Creases and wrinkles we want to hide
Old age will inevitably fire its missile
And no one escapes its fearless glide

The natural differences in all Mankind
God suited with skin color and hair
Along man brought his excess baggage
Under a shrouding and beauteous snare

To remodel and alter our very existence
Traps our essence in a stranglehold
For a likeness God created the human form
But crafted parts for our own unique mould

With such daring efforts to disguise
Or demean our unique marks of birth
Is this tug of war with Mother Nature
Defying God and our own self worth?

(2005)

The Spirited Guests

Silently wondering of another presence
When I felt the gush of a chill
Since my home was not being shared
I tried ignoring the eerie feel

Thinking things were missing or mislaid
When clearly untouched by me
Something or someone had reign of my home
As a spirit I could feel but never see

Occasionally hearing a foreign voice
At times even sounds of laughter
Not to mention the bumping noises
As if someone's being chased after

I'd hear creaking noises on the upstairs floor
And footsteps mounting the stairs
Just after the sound of a squeaking door
Was the trudging of a second pair

History surfaced of the previous tenants
That none had the bravery to stay
Haunting in this house was never revealed
A selling feature…one would hardly say

Further searching the building's curious past
In their bed two young lovers were killed
Revelations succeeding in jangling my nerves
Of their antics I'd had my fill

These creepy lovebirds were getting their thrills
Playing their teasing tricks of the dead
But their gory abode quickly lost its appeal
And raised the last hair on my head

(2004)

The Hood Unveiled

Their escape is to surrender or be damned
A plight penetrating all seasons
Unconscionable war upon their existence
Where pity's exhausted all reasons

Human bondage has caused irreparable harm
That's mercilessly beyond repair
Bones, bellies and lily-white eyes
Forever cloaked in a hollow stare

Atrocities unveil their hood of suffering
An existence in shallow dispute
The unnatural journey into the silence
Of closed mouths and ears like mutes

Tyrants unleashed their unlawful tirade
Of death upon camp after camp
In a nation of games, blame...unspeakable shame...
Lives indelible prints of war stamps

(1999)

Season's End

Summer ends as its beauty fades
And much of its foliage turns brown
Fall swings in with a show of its own
In a colorful and sporty crown

Cropping is nearing the end of its harvest
Of fruits and vegetables to bear
Leaves are constantly gracing the ground
From the past seasons' wear and tear

Creatures have made their way underground
And some have even flown south
They're in exile 'til nature notifies
With signals rivaling word of mouth

As trees settle into their twilight phase
Their leaves now mulching the ground
The annihilation of winter is welcome
As the theatrics of spring abounds

(2002)

The Boarding House

On the comer of Third and Elm
Sits a house of Victorian style
As midnight life becomes quiet and still
Peace settles in for a while

Every comer of the earth acquaints
Its uniqueness in some young girl
With every imaginable ethnic descent
Comes styles from around the world

Passing daily, with a chat or smile
Some would sit cheerfully and converse
Others would join in a campus walk
Spouting views in broken verse

Strolling the hall at a leisurely pace
I see two of these women embrace
Then quickly retreating within themselves
Upon glimpsing my curious face

Downstairs, beneath the residence hall
There's a laundry for clothing care
Upstairs, a salon is filled with the chatter
Of those shampooing and dressing hair

Most have come to seek fame or fortune
In a city of opportunity and appeal
While each struggle to find their niche
Few will have their dreams fulfilled

(1998)

Nigger

Foolish tongues will utter words
And think there's nothing wrong
Choosing to rendezvous with indifference
By packaging them poetically in a song

Comedic attempts to entertain the masses
With the fun they're deemed to poke
Loosely spouting words of degradation
To an audience well beyond the jokes

Pouring salt in this open wound
We've tried through the years to heal
"Nigger" they say is just a word
Expressing what the artist feels

"My nigger" some say is endearing
Though sounding much like the claim
Whites made feeling supreme with ownership
Of their "nigras" they so aptly named

A slur that continues hanging like a noose
Around those nescient necks
Feeds the appetite of the racist rogues
Content with disrespect

Embracing and promoting such an image
With a history of derogatory fame
Enhances the degradation of all people
By continuing to enforce its shame

One's privilege of hoarding this "black" brand
Claiming the right to authorize its use

Assures those using it without permission
Is charged with racial abuse

Enslaving society to such ignorance
A tradition that should have long been broken
Shouting or spouting "nigger" in speech or song
From any mouth should never be spoken

(2008)

Winter Madness

A canopy of tin as the covered roof
Its heat fled quietly with the sun
As the cold wind ushered in with fury
Another chilly night's journey had begun

Wind drafts penetrated the old oak walls
Through cracks and fissures aligned
The weather was ripe for parching skin
And spanking scarcely covered behinds

Smothered and unable to turn in comfort
Beneath quilts heavily heaped on the bed
A dare to leave your home without
Something to cover your back or head

Knotholes firmly exerted their position
To impress the linoleum on the floor
Against the wall stood a potbellied stove
And nails mounted to hang coats on the door

With an ample supply of wood to burn
Piled high on a shaky incline
Winter madness was threatening its coldest year
As the winds became quietly benign

(2004)

Birthrights

These simple joys are soon to fade
As you anxiously herald my birth
Years will pass with furtive opportunity
To frame or distort my worth

I am not to be a celebrated gift
That's just for recognition and praise
And I'm not a package that can be returned
So wrap me with love as I'm raised

There's great expense in my happiness
Trying to satisfy each and every need
Be cautious in preparing me for the world
Unattended I'm just like a weed

Heed the nurturing bond between us
As our days will be tirelessly long
I'll need from you an ironclad promise
That you'll teach me right from wrong

Given the flashing light on my rights
You should listen to what I have to say
But your advantage as parent is to stay in charge
And make sure as a child I obey

(1992)

Elephant Ears

I heard them talking…
And laughing, when Mama called Daddy
A cheating, sorry-ass old prick
Said she'd been trying for years to figure out
What made the old geezer tick

I heard them talking…
Mama and one of her friends
About some floozy Daddy had found
Now she knows what's been keeping him
And why he stopped coming around

I heard them talking…
When I peeked through the window
Mama laughed, saying she hated the old fart
Does that mean she hates me too
When she says we're like peas in a pod?

I heard them talking…
Mama caught and scolded me
For watching her and a friend getting dressed
God, she said, would punish prying eyes
And to stop, or I'd never be blessed

Listen…I hear them…
Mama and Daddy whispering
To be careful saying things we shouldn't hear
Though she knows that I'm somewhere listening
With my big, nosey…elephant… ears

(2004)

Foolish Pleasures

Old men lost in backyard confessions
Eagerly explore the drama in their lives
A snapshot of who's married and who's living in
Was my invitation to dateless jive

Applauding accomplishments of every child
Hinting bittersweet emotions for their wives
Some moaned of having to manage daily needs
And how hard it's getting to survive

One jokes of keeping his woman happy
Never bothering to say with what
But blames her for making unnecessary bills
And causing the corners he's having to cut

A friend boasts about his high school love
And her leniency in having their baby boy
Bragging, there's no pressure for money or marriage
Since she knows that baby's his joy

One old man stood rocking on his heels
Out of the blue began spinning his tale
Confides the foolish pleasures he's had with women
Has only made his life pure hell

Six children he has at home with his wife
Squashing rumors of two others outside
Struggling to provide for family at home
The others he successfully hides

With piercing eyes staring straight at me
Spouting testimony seemed only for my ears

As he talked it was becoming quite clear
He was driving home reality fears

I never wanted that many children, he said
And not one of them came with a plan
Forced to marry without a grip on life
Just robbed me of being my own man

The fellas joke that it's a rich legacy
To carry on a family name
But my past will only leave my family
Heavy baggage and unnecessary shame

Spreading seeds, my son, won't make you a man
And there's one thing you need to learn
Babies will arrive whether planned or not
Demanding their share of what you earn

(2008)

The Blues Migration

The blues migration flows
With watchers among the fray
A prompt or poke from the butt of a gun
Its barrel pointing the way
The looming fear of death is thick
For a glance, or crossed look
A jab for a slight motion or tick
A guard unwittingly mistook

The blues migration flows
Allowing little time to grieve
The price for freedom shrouds this journey
Be killed, or without arise, leave
Is the next township poised
To extend a welcome hand
To an exodus mired in such chaos
Seeking solace on foreign land?

The blues migration flows
In spurts of shadows filled with woes
Of the innocent who's mowed down
And the weak with spirit lows
Heads crowned with heavy loads
Over tracks from shoeless feet
A moment to relieve the tired and weary
Parking baggage for resting seats

The blues migration flows
Under a covenant of fear
With heavy hearts and broken dreams
As eyes bleed swollen tears
Can there be salvation ahead

In an uncertain path of gloom
Or just another compromising
Shield for impending doom?

(2009)

The Campfire Girl

The doorbell rings…
With a smile she stands
Those spindly legs
Propped in tennis feet
A ladder of boxes
Spills from the hands
Of this freckled face
With silver-laced teeth

She scampers across
Every lawn on the block
Peddling goods
From her private stock
In a frantic race
Tempting…teasing…and shoving
Her skill of cookie power
In every sucker's face

She's keeping alive
A tradition of cheer
With mammoth consumption
And little calorie fear
A population of cells
That's gallantly slipping…
Sliding…and wallowing
In their own fat hell

Before the crispy crème
Chanced touting itself
As the world's guilty
Pleasure of choice
This campfire girl's

Irresistible weapon
Spoke volumes for icons
Without a voice

(2002)

The Ivory Moon

The ivory moon is full and rising
In and out of the rolling clouds
An evening left cooled by the setting sun
And a crimson glow hanging like a shroud

Passion steals the night's serenity
As our romance tries kicking a start
The moon's brilliance has settled in ivory
Peeking in on our floundering hearts

Its stone face glares at the eve of night
As our emotions sputter to a race
Growing darkness looms all around
Insisting on sharing its grace

Dazzling stars play hide and seek
So the moon cannot see their beauty
Capriciously abandoning all lovers tonight
By cheating and neglecting their duty

The stars radiance continues to shine
On this balmy night in late June
The midnight haze that stole their splendor
Left a gleam of the ivory moon

(2010)

The Hideaway

Sold in chains
To work cotton fields
Harriet mapped her plans
Leading her people by will

With no other way
To give them the news
Her messages she sang
In coded clues

Passing out old clothes
Worn and tattered shoes
A small comfort or satisfaction
In curbing their blues

Barking and yelping dogs
Sniffing and chasing her trail
Were hard to outrun
But she didn't dare fail

Leading her people
In the darkest of night
They trekked for miles
Underground and out of sight

The morning sun rose
Glistening through the trees
Another day of hope
They'd escaped without a breeze

(2005)

A Commoner's Journey

Feeling burdened and lost in direction
And needing to heal the soul
Laying all troubles at the Master's feet
Allows them to freely unfold

The eyes will plead to bleed their tears
Refrain and let them flow
Entitle the heart its full release
When feelings are willing to show

Leave vanity, titles and honors at the door
When identifying who you are
God's not impressed with all the fanfare
Only in your eyes you're a star

Identify your need and your trouble
If it's what you brought to share
A plea for redemption in a simple prayer
The rest, God doesn't care

We're all on a commoner's journey
Coming before him as we are
He knows all the troubles surrounding us
After watching both near and far

(2007)

I Never Flinched

I stand alone, unarmed
Silent and confused
Lingering in life without alarm
A hundred years used and abused

Accused of blocking another's view
They came with slashing blades
While I was thinking all along
I was just throwing shade

The slashers return every year
To inflict their painful pinch
All because I've overlapped
Their aim is to make me flinch

Surprised I stand in eclipse
Stripped bare of all my leaves
The elements of nature pushed furiously
Trying to bring me to my knees

Cloaked in the wind's intensive fury
My cover is wrestled to the ground
Now I'm as naked as a newborn
Yet still can't make a sound

Without cover, in the cold I stand
Not needing a summer trim
Exposed to all of nature's wrath
That showed up on a whim

Others raise their limbs against me
To leave soothing signs of claim

Again I wasn't allowed to flinch
As they struck with perfect aim

I see the loggers coming again
I'm hoping, for another tree
As they grew closer, I managed to flinch
But they insisted on tagging me

(2010)

Rambling Rose

Rose…A fair-haired, fun-loving girl
Akin to a sixties wildflower
Garbed in colorful and dowdy attire
She was known for keeping late hours

Grown into a woman of all seasons
A liberated and outspoken voice
How she's portrayed, and for any reason
She became who she was by choice

Rose slowly began to lose her appeal
No longer as hot as she thought
Becoming a hollow shell of a woman
On her health snuck a creeping assault

A prayer, she'd recite day by day
Through a friend she'd begun seeking help
Fighting to curb the vicious outbreak
Trespassing on her body with welts

Morphed as a victim of her own passions
Finding pleasure with the wild and bold
Engaging in daring fads and fun
While vices were ravaging her soul

The epitome of a wide-eyed child
Often warned of how she behaved
Engaging in wild and reckless behavior
Tilting her toward an early grave

But Rose was tough and resilient to the end
Fighting a viral scourge of pain
Many thought she'd finally found her way
As this little girl died in vain

(2009)

Nails in the Sand

Mystery engulfed a sleepy little town
When a young woman vanished in thin air
Police and family had no leads or theory
Of what happened Saturday night at the fair

An enduring fantasy for a life in the city
Fuelled gossip she'd run off with a man
But leaving family and friends without notice
Just wasn't the behavior of little Anne

Last seen on the arm of her longtime beau
Foot dragging compromised any clues
Failing to call or report her missing
Was strange behavior for a man in his blues

Weeks became months and months became years
As the case of little Anne grew cold
Even fellow officers dismissed the suspicions
A brother of theirs would be so bold

As a noonday hiker on a stroll through the woods
Noticed a weathered bag in the sand
A careless kick unearthed an old crime
When out popped a nail-painted hand

Police poured in to process the scene
The bumbling sheriff showed up as well
A nightmare for some family brought home to rest
Remains of one who'd been through hell

Identified as Anne who seemed much alive
As dirt was being thrown in her face

Reaching, and trying to claw her way out
What was to become her resting place

Tried, found guilty and convicted of murder
Her man served barely two years time
In this red clay town where the boys in blue
Were known to cover and weasel out of crimes

A case dealing such a miscarriage of justice
Grossly overshadowed the family's grief
Worse than handing a sick dog a dry bone
Is solving a murder that provides no relief

(2008)

The Abyss

Adrift on this sinking ship
Is there a warning or voice I should hear
Signs that speak within my realm
Without penetrating my nerves
With fear

If I could
Have spoken to an ancestor
Before inheriting their profane ways
And had the courage to ask them why
Their hate's not a passing phase

They've left me hating so many
That I don't know…and frankly never met
Where's the hope for those to follow
As the past continues
Raising its head

I am the new generation
That's thrust into this black hole
An abyss of ancestral hatred
An inheritance
Consuming my soul

This abyss to many is invisible
As I hang in its balance by a thread
Forever brazened
Upon an unarmed heart
Pity the virgin brains to be fed

(2012)

The Coffin Filler

Holding court with the serene and silent
Who, for a few days would never leave
Sharing dark and dreary quarters to put up
Any guest expecting the bereaved

A somber journey consumed in grief
To a getaway that's eerie and cold
Loose shingles on the roof flapped and flopped
As hard as the angry wind blowed

Caskets shadowed the empty walls
Their satin linings beckoning to be filled
The wild-eyed mortician harnessed a fear
In a face with an icy chill

Best in the business at covering his deeds
And one never to make a mess
Behind locked doors he would make his rounds
Before starting his funeral dress

Appeasing the gurgling noise of any corpse
Assumed to be already dead
Obliging them with a thump to the chest
Or a tap on the back of the head

Peeled back and packed as sturdy as stone
Bodies as chilled as the slab where they laid
Awaiting the confines of a cozy coffin
Which breathless souls had been slain?

(2007)

The Soapbox

Snow is privileged to ravage your day
A nightmare, when you're planning to fly
Don't blame anyone else…blame me
But don't come asking me why

Birds you don't see out and about
And their life's order is to fly
Knowing that snow is part of my plan
Today, most don't even try

And me…! I have plans of my own
That I'll never get around to
Listening all morning to the whines and issues
Of so many others like you

I showed up early to set the stage
And you're already on your soapbox
I've watched you acting up, front and center
With so little time on my clock

The shows that you've been putting on
It's out that you're all the rage
Seeing your best performance today
Is all I ask while gracing my stage

I invited you here for many reasons
For everyone to have their say
I'm sorry if you weren't advised
We're closing in on Judgment Day

Now, you'll find as we go along
For many things I must take the credit
Today, what I'll witness from you
Determines my final edit

While you're bragging about building the car
You must remember I showed you how
And that technology you say is changing the world
You've become too dependent on now

Needing a product with mass appeal
You designed and produced the gun
But I've only seen you use it to kill
Surely you're not calling that fun

And that airplane…! What an invention!
Now there's a reason to be proud
But without me, and my stratosphere
It would never make it in the clouds

Remember your reasons for being on stage
Is only about the good you do
I don't need to hear shallow excuses
Of what others have done to you

You're never to mention another's plight
Unless it's who you robbed or killed
This for you should be an easy confession
I've noticed you boast with little skill

I already know about the forest trees
That you've pulled out of the soil
The number of underground wells you've drained
And the misuses of their oil

The forests you've robbed of their resources
And its dwellers you caused to flee
You did know having to answer for that
Is the reason you're facing me

Still lost...? Stop and think for a moment
What I ask of you—on my terms
I'm actually here to motivate you
So you may want to listen and learn

I can, and will, often change the seasons
Since this is my world at large
There are things you're doing to alter them
But never forget who's in charge

We both know there's behavior on earth
As pure evil continues to surge
With so much chaos, discord and confusion
At some point it has to be purged

I've provided this place for all to gather
So everyone has freedom to play
You, like many others, can't see my purpose
Until your judgment day

Problems...? I know, I've seen them all
Black, white and those in-between
Though you still hate, fight and even kill each other
For humans...such unbecoming scenes

Now, I'll hear about all the others
You took from because you could
Never stopping to think what you took from them
In the end does you no good

About those children you failed to raise
And their mother you freely abused
I know…she's yours and you refuse to let her go
Because control is consuming you

You've had time and chance to live and learn
But you never seemed to care
Now you're asking me to forget your sins
And a room in my home you want to share?

(2005)

Peace

We must seek ways to coexist
In a world of uncommon grounds
Never looking, acting or thinking the same
In most of us good can be found

God shows us there is a need for prayer
For hope and faith in mankind
To preserve and share existence on his land
In this world of yours and mine

We can surpass the doubts and fears
Of the future and where it leads
By shaking the poison from our souls
Upon which hatred feeds

Peace is possible when we respect
And learn what it means to embrace
Instead of turning our back and neglecting those
Of a different faith or race

When hatred is allowed to man the controls
Peace pulls away from the dock
Escaping from our minds and souls
As a misplaced war on God's clock

(1998)

Judge and Fury

As Mama was putting dinner on the table
And we were sitting down to eat
Through the window a dark hovering cloud
Was a stranger we dared to meet

The wind whistled fiercely, as it was turning
The afternoon as dark as night
A mountainous whirlwind looming in the distance
Was churning its way in full sight

Mama quickly returned dinner to the stove
With a promise to eat a little later
Pop mumbled a prayer that we'd still be alive
As we braced to greet a tornado

Dropping his paper beside the chair
He rose to examine the coming fury
Grabbing and pulling us away from the window
On our town swooped judge and fury

Seeing objects whirling through the air
Hearing others blowing around outside
The tornado, as it moved closer in
Was spreading its winds pretty wide

For a while, somewhere all around town
Screaming sirens invaded the streets
We were herded for safety into a back room
A relatively dark and airless retreat

Quietly watching family faces in fear
And listening to the violence outside

In a matter of minutes the storm was taking
Our emotions on a perilous ride

Soon, daylight began to surface again
But things outside looked pretty grim
Seeing clearly through a blown-out window
What had come and gone in a whim

Emerging to safety with our roof partly gone
It too, had been claimed in the violence
We surveyed the scene, stunned and amazed
Wandering around engulfed in silence

A car rested against a ravaged tree
With a leak somewhere loudly hissing
A ramshackle coop that sat behind the house
Was gone and all of our chickens missing

Some homes stood with roofs blown off
For many the whole structures were gone
Others were left with only foundations
But untouched, two stood eerily alone

(1994)

Disasters

Disasters are armed to strike with fear
Leaving us with nowhere to hide
While some allows time to prepare for safety
Others take us on a devastating ride

We cling to a relative degree of ignorance
Of the reason disasters strike
Our earth is crowned in such disarray
And drawn into its mightiest fights

Mother Nature comes cloaked in many forms
And she's showing up for good reason
Not always knocking before coming in
With keys in hand for any season

Whether she appears in the dead of night
Or charts a slow, steady course by day
Whatever her reason for showing up
It's a cue to get out of her way

If a weakened dam or levee breaks
Did we simply dismiss its warning?
Or in the wake of a brewing storm
Ignore the alarm before its dawning?

In amazement, as victims we often express
When surveying a disaster's aftermath
Needing and desiring to build something stronger
Learn nothing's storm-proof in God's path

Tragedy presents us our own unique hurdles
Often leaving our feelings shattered
With time to examine our faith and goodwill
And to review in our lives what really matters

(2005)

A Lady Scorned

She lay peacefully among flapping tongues
Cloaked in an ivory satin gown
A veil of secrecy shrouded the holy room
As gossip was claiming its crown

Rumors circled around her demise
Revealing details of a life aborted
But many held on, astounded and denying
The news they found so sordid

Idle cliques blanketed the thirsty lawn
Inside, mourners packed the pews
The curious gawked, while hugging the walls
Swapping rumors and hospital news

The bereaved ushered in and down the aisle
Past an attentive but somber crowd
A few steps beyond the open casket
Raw emotions spilled out loud

The scorn, as infinite as her silence
Robbed family of a guiltless escape
While witnessing doctors treat a minor illness
A fury of poisons directed her fate

A family left struggling and regretting
How a life of hopes and dreams slipped away
Mere happiness, youth and promise pushed aside
In the absence of a suitable mate

(1975)

A Semblance of Light

Out of the darkness of apartheid
Emerged a semblance of unfettered light
Praise cloaked the heart of a benefactor
That rose to champion this fight

Young girls, underprivileged in many ways
Were granted wishes they had only dreamed
Unshackled, to ride the great horizon
To a life they'd never seen

Grasping hearts were poised to criticize
As benevolence was smudged and attacked
Should joy in this celebration be denied
While jealousy and envy cloud the facts

Peace and splendor will mold these lives
And desires, when determined to succeed
To abolish an endless strife for those
With a fervor outweighing others' greed

Ignoring the vicious voices singing off-key
To resound the trumpets and horns
One looks blindly at what the world needs
Seeking silence where leaders are born

(2007)

A Walk in Space

I hoofed through the streets like a stallion
Streets that I knew were unsafe
But if I was in my bed asleep
Could it be just a walk in space?

I crossed one rooftop to another
Yet I never made a step out of place
But if I was in my bed asleep
It must have been a walk in space

I swam the lake with my baby brother
Against him I could never keep pace
But if I was in my bed asleep
Was it just another walk in space?

If these adventures are all common
They are surely uncommon on their face
They're things I wouldn't ordinarily do
If in reality it's without a trace

Extending thanks for guarding my safety
As I slept in these foreign places
I cannot deny that it must have been
My God! I was saved by your grace

(2011)

The Jury Is Out

An old man sits, reading his book
An old lady begins to knit

A thug shifts restlessly in baggy pants
While an actor practices his skit

One young man is engaged on the phone
Another who is late rushes in

A juror scolds her youngster at home
While another lotions her skin

One juror steps out for a smoker's break
While another sits down to eat

Jurors eleven and twelve engage in talking sports
As they've wasted no time to meet

If a juror's task is deciding one's fate
We must wonder about their focus and vision

When so absorbed in their own affairs
Can they reach fair and just decisions?

(2006)

Father's Day

I often looked to you with my problems
To quick fix a random need

Like spotting me with a few dollars for school
Or handing over your car keys

I always thought you had plenty of money
When you said you didn't have it to give

Claiming you'd already given it to Mama
So we could eat and have a place to live

But I was too young to know or even care
So I'd like to apologize

Now that I'm older and out on my own
Survival has opened my eyes

Lately, I've found it's just nice to hang out
Maybe go for a neighborhood walk

To catch up on what's happening with you
Or just to have a father-daughter talk

(1996)

Ignor-Ancy

Easily, I read their fair faces
Upon my walking in
Indeed humanity became the prey
In this parody of a lion's den

As evil eyes were stalking me
Stealthily I walked past
The clerks never parted conversation
Ignored, I was aghast

Inching upon an attitude
Battling Mama's learning curve
They'd found the perfect candidate
That loathed such display of nerve

Lifting a pricey purse from the wall
Above a "do not touch" display
"What can I help you with?" one asked
"We're short of help today"

A deliberate survey around the room
Fuelled me to have my say
"You have no customers in your store"
Good help, it's rumored you won't pay

Encountering a problem attitude
I was never one to scream and shout
But never allowed to be disrespected
Without cursing someone out

But I summoned grace with dignity
Though I'd been greeted wrong
With evil thoughts coursing my mind
God had to be holding my tongue

(2009)

Liberation

Drowning daily in this fermented pound
Pondering my fate in a hell without sound
None know of my life but a greater source
How I should handle this negative force

I close my eyes, though I rarely sleep
Rising in the morning, worn, wearied and beat
Longing for freedom is a pressing hunger
As each passing day stretches a little longer

I call out for help, but can only hear
My own weary voice echoing in my ear
Vivid images that my eyes cannot see
Are thoughts of freedom embedded in me

These hollow cries of distress and sorrow
Entwines me in much confusion
I see the timely and curious eyes of a matron
Prescribed, but a harassing intrusion

At worse, I am obsessed and driven
In a conflict of cruelty and fear
Trying to unravel the course of my sins
And the senseless reasons I'm here

(1989)

Social Illusions

She was bold and brash
With a studded tongue
And a silver ring in her nose

He was rather fancy
On loud hippie girls
Dressed in sassy tie-dyed clothes

He wore a Mohawk
With pierced ears
His body laced in garish tattoos

She was drawn
To loud pompous men
Short in stature wearing platform shoes

Conveniently married to an older man
A daddy sponsor
Clad in leisure suits

Her open infidelity
With a younger man
Soon earned the old coot the boot

Her goal as benefactor
To ailing children
Was to shower them with toys

His money and image
Provided power and cover
Of outside-the-law decoys

Harleys, bandanas and cowboy boots
And an underground
Pipeline of drugs

Somehow these charitable
Icons had managed
To elude the reputation of thugs

(2002)

Heartstrings

A child who tends to anger his parents
As he stumbles and makes mistakes

A parent should be that child's anchor
No matter how long it takes

A wife may say no to her husband
Yet bend him like a hook

She's prone to analyze his daily habits
Of most she chooses to overlook

A restless mate will sometimes cheat
Without giving it a second thought

Embracing the thrill of a one-time fling
And feelings of not getting caught

The presence of stale, unfamiliar scents
And strands of foreign hair

In a pinch one is prone to lie
To cover an illicit affair

A husband and wife should remember
Their vows and promise to forsake

And be aware for peace and harmony
The amount of patience it takes

Emotions and feelings we all harbor
On which our love ones tug

This extra baggage on the heartstrings
From day to day we lug

(2003)

Homew* ork

Just out of bed
Homework you must do
Yes, even for someone
As little as you

A bath you should've taken
The night before
Often not enough time
For mornings on the go

Washing face and hands
Combing and brushing hair
This, you must learn
For when Mom's not there

Brushing your teeth
Up, down and around
A thorough cleansing
Keeps them healthy and sound

First meal of the day
Should be more than a treat
A balanced breakfast
Is what you should eat

Pants pulled up
And held with a belt
Your frame looks neater
Even smart and svelte

Dresses, skirts and
Pants of any kind

Should never be worn
To expose your behind

Wrinkles in your clothes
You should always press
Never leave your home
Unless properly dressed

(2007)

J.J.'s Surprise

Christmas morning little J.J. came alive
Searching with anxious eyes

Knowing that somewhere under the tree
A box held a special surprise

Tearing away colorful ribbons and wrap
That's hiding this gift within

Others watch, their jaws dropping
As J.J's disappointment begins

His eyes drooped sadly, his smile disappeared
As wonder passed over the room

From all around came efforts to cheer
Little J.J. out of his gloom

Pouting, he shoved the box aside
"I don't want G.I. Joe," he said

Family suspicions came home to roost
It should have been Barbie instead

(1983)

Invisible Wings

A spirit promises boundless riches
If one is to trust and obey

Consumed in a black hole of misery
To fail you in some way

This master of disguise is joked to frolic
In red, pointed ears and a tail

It's easy to succumb and buy into
What he is peddling for sale

He preys on and convinces the weak
Revealing only what they need to see

Some are wooed and conned by this rogue
Accepting what he masks as free

Eagerly donning those invisible wings
Many marvel at what he brings

Delivering his message in the smoothest talk
Even in a voice he may sing

Costumed...not in red and without pointed ears
And no tail as his presence unfolds

Neither will you see wings on this creature
As he sets out to steal your soul

(2000)

Breeding Ground

Eden, though nearly three years old
Doting parents find reasons to coo
Ignoring other children with a host of needs
Seems neither of them knows what to do

Unruly children running wild and free
Feeling privileged to do as they please
Their reckless behavior with no consequences
Wreck feelings and property with ease

Dad escapes in silence behind his paper
Ignoring precious time to bond
Mom's duties of chauffer, cook and housekeeper
Leaves her little time to respond

As children indulged in every whim
Allowing disastrous behavior to breed
Parents failing to recognize a need from a want
Surrenders to an ever-mounting greed

A lack of discipline and self-control
Often land children socially out of place
Neglecting to harness unruly behavior
Looms a destiny of failure and disgrace

The inherent freedom in every child
Does not permit to control or take over
Tame and temper their behavior early on
Or become prisoner providing their cover

(1998)

Best Man Stand'n

The guests waited cozily in their seats
As the father strolled in with the bride
Two young girls raising a canopy of lace
Trailed gracefully stride for stride

The groom, known for his tardiness
Appeared earlier, but left the affair
When word leaked that he'd walked away
Emotions descended into despair

The mother fainted upon hearing the news
As the father stood fit to be tied
The bride trembled in shame and contempt
For whom she'd trusted and relied

Guests sat mumbling under their breath
Most stunned in horror and wonder
Where the groom's deceptive heart and mistrust
Led the feelings he'd chosen to squander

Stood up, and left alone at the altar
No groom…a wedding went on as planned
With romance never missing in the room
To the rescue was the groom's best man

Stepping in, with eagerness to please
And comforting the bride in her anger
While raising curiosity among the guests
She was taking no friendly stranger

(2009)

Bridges

The same tongue lashing out insults
Can just as loudly spout praise
With efforts to respect outside one's realm
Communication levels are raised

Friction wanders loosely among the lost
Erecting permanent hedges of defense
The blood of brotherhood flows aimlessly
Where denied glory in life is immense

Does one expect a peaceful world
Where tradition buries the joy of life?
With discord plaguing the unsettled heart
No change brings freedom without strife

When building bridges to coexist
Only peace and goodwill's the common ground
Regardless of race, color, creed or religion
Around us all God's arms surround

(1998)

The Crippled Spines

The strength of two towers claimed in the night
And bent into weeping pines
Their limbs drooped like those of a willow
From ice that crippled their spine

An overnight visit of predicted frost
Left needles sheathed in heavy ice
The trees, taking their bow in silence
Had paid nature's ultimate price

In the sun, they continued to cower
Powerless, and damaged beyond repair
Sheared needles gracefully blanketing the ground
Shined and glistened like angel hair

The plight of these trees was a testament
Of how Mother Nature forces her hand
Never warning that rain was part of her plan
Again thwarting the forecast of man

(1975)

The Intruder

As a cool, breezy summer's eve
Faded beneath a crimson sky
A stranger awaiting my return
Stood still as I passed by

I flashed a glance upon his face
But this he never knew
My heart raced, my legs went limp
In fear of what he'd do

Concealing himself under the stairs
As I trekked them one by one
The stranger, in his utter silence
Sparked fears I'd never known

Inside, as I thrust the door shut
Exhausted, but my safety prevailed
With the stranger outside, and me within
My fears were somewhat curtailed

Flinging my purse in its usual spot
In a corner of the couch
Sitting down to ease my aching feet
Fatigue forced me into a nodding slouch

Awakened in a flash, to a creaking door
And soft steps of cautious feet
I waited with silent anticipation
For the stranger I dared to meet

There in the darkness I lay quiet and still
As he silhouetted my door

My body drowning in beads of sweat
Fear pumped my heart once more

In a strong Woodbury scent he stood
Gazing silently over my frame
With a racing heart, his intent I pondered
Like prey in a hunter's game

He stepped forward for a closer look
Flashing a light upon my face
As I leaped in a rage of screaming fear
He dashed in a frantic pace

Relieved that I had escaped the wrath
And violation of my space
I pondered the path of this meddlesome punk
And where next he'd show his face

(1982)

Silent Creeper

Your thirst for power reeked of danger
As a creature creeping out to steal
Sipping the breath of all you came near
Just hoping science failed to heal

Taking the liberty to surface at will
When in spirit I was not at my best
Though your presence was bittersweet
You were hardly a welcome guest

Unable to escape from under your cloud
Without the manpower of a team
My aim and goal was to slow you down
Before you could emerge full steam

Receiving with hesitation a lifesaving drip
Imagining how to make the process quicker
My refuge was an unforgiving nap
Awaking only to find myself sicker

Many days I stopped, looking into a mirror
And wondered how the stranger staring back
With sallow skin, sparse and thinning hair
Managed somehow to throw you off track

Remiss, I hoped never to see you again
But I'll think of you as I grow old
Carrying with me a peace within
That you're gone from my body and soul

(2002)

The Fortune Hunter

Stifling desires of this blushing bride
On board, a match of prudent stealth

But will her family man be unveiled
Before he can squander her wealth

The benefit of riches he's never known
So his position he tries to advance

With her family sandwiched in between
There's hardly an available chance

Many of his intentions are easily thwarted
Each day in their wedded bliss

There's always the presence of someone lurking
Or intruding on an attempted kiss

In all of his planning, he had not expected
Such tight-fisted family control

Someone is always on guard of his actions
And the security of his bride's bankroll

Now that he's aware that his road to riches
Is a distressing and bumpy ride

He's not equipped to take over a fortune
That's not in the control of his bride

Call it love, he contends with some affection
Claiming passion at the forefront

He bows out quietly without any objection
Another rogue on a fortune hunt

(2002)

The Prophet's Profit

The prophet often strayed from home
Leaving his loving wife to care
Or fill some poor old ailing lady's
Request for a needed prayer

He'd travel miles through the night
To reach the next town to address
An adoring crowd awaited his arrival
Admittedly just to press his flesh

Never hanging around in any place longer
Than to bask in his flock's affection
He'd meet, greet and preach a quick sermon
Then pass his plate for collection

His wife, when present, was the perfect host
For his lacking in social grace
And covering his most dastardly deeds
Of missing funds the Church couldn't trace

His dearest alliance sought upon his death
The wife was asked to claim his remains
But the fleeting spiritual room in her heart
Abandoned ashes that provided no gains

(2004)

The Learning Curve

Difficulties, setbacks and disappointments
I've faced day in and day out
I try to see these as learning curves
Of what life is all about

It never promises happiness
Or freedom from hurt or pain
There are times I have to remind myself
Losses can be profits or gains

Forgetting what's been lost
Or how often I've been burned
I can channel my thoughts on moving on
And focus on what I've learned

When left to dwell on acceptance
I'm not always at my best
But I try to take rejection to mean
That I've been truly blessed

I try to claim my blessings
Wherever they may be
Knowing they come at times and places
The naked eye don't always see

(2004)

The Stargazer

As the door opened
In breezed the honored guest
With glittering jewels
Adorning her chest

She strolled with ease
And a fiendish flair
Her head lifted high
With a guarded air

A glare in her eyes
Like bubbles of glass
Men stared intently
As she crossed their paths

She smiled with lips
So filled with tease
They'd nod covertly
Her looks so pleased

Alone with husbands
Wives feared she'd steal
Only her presence
Could expose these heels

They'd have her mingle
Any way they could
But to have her own man
Wives thought she should

(2002)

The Opaque Bubble

What's in a culture
Where bad behavior
Is rewarded and glorified

Where claims of good
Moral character is boring
And socially denied

The lives of privilege
Seems celebrated from
The outside looking in

A sign of hollow
Enduring standards
With an emptiness in the end

When shallow lives
Are out of control
They often end up in trouble

Often, admiring and unsuspecting
Youth will fail
To see inside this bubble

(2002)

Heroes

A call to service I wasn't pleased
But tried to handle it with a bit of ease

Told this war was now my job
Deep down I felt I was getting robbed

If this is a burden that I must bear
Buy me armor to show you care

Design me a helmet that's mortar proof
To protect my head from the enemy troops

A shield for my chest wherever I go
To mind the dangers whether high or low

Within this war and at its best
It's hardly anything but a character test

As bullets, missiles and mortars fly
My soul dies a little as they whiz by

The allied trust of service women and men
Shallow reasons for war is not a nurtured trend

If the country's honor is to be maintained
Loyalty must be abiding and so ingrained

But are we so praised as brave defenders
In a senseless war we refuse to surrender

The rhetoric to us you continue to feed
When the toll of suffering has gone beyond deed

(2005)

Penny Savers

The indulging ways we cry and complain
When a meal is absent a day
Diminishes the suffering surrounding us
That for many is life's cruel way

Trekking miles to draw water from a stream
That is often too dirty to drink
For pennies on the dollar this needed source
Can be provided for less than we think

Poverty in the lives of our fellow man
For some will never change an ounce
The daily task of going without
Is a condition we must simply denounce

Shattered beginnings often robs a life
That struggles to make amends
From every pocket of the Universe
This battle of hopelessness we can win

(1991)

A Man in Mind

Never mind a man
that open doors

Cherish the one
that scrubs the floors

A man that likes
and knows how to cook

But takes time also
to read a book

A man that spends time
with his child

Who doesn't mind
and does it with a smile

A man that's capable
of taking a stand

But one that's conscious
of his tempered hand

Now, I don't mind a man
who wants to protect

But I won't have one
that gives no respect

(1987)

The Relay

Hearing the thoughts of our mind
Some heed while others choose to run
Though it is hardly the intention of any child
To hold on to everything they learn

The investing task of raising a child
Reckless discipline lends a lifetime of abuse
As society braces to inherit them later
We must watch how we turn them loose

Chaos breeds darkness in their lives
And we can only hope it doesn't last
If it's delivered in candor without caution
Their behavior is the baton we've passed

(2005)

The Competition

You shouted the loudest, spirited cheers
And you're in doubt of making the squad
You're the best ever there is on the team
But cut for a bad report card

You've listened all day to your instructor shout
On your technique she continues to harp
You learn you've been cut from the troupe
Though your dance moves are crisp and sharp

To find out you didn't make the team
And you've practiced the hardest every day
Listening to your coaches enduring screams
Even second string you failed to make

You're told now there's a price for being late
A space you lost for that reason
There's no way to explain away local traffic
Only time can master this treason

You calculate the price for just being you
Excuses of simple song and dance
You'll find life's not always a fair competition
Even for those most deserving the chance

(2008)

War Games

Unlawful intrusions before our eyes
A calm fear runs the house of our nation
Among twisted views and hands of greed
Like those of a slave plantation

Bearing witness to a gamut of fumbles
Of the over-aged and out of control
Faux and padded popularity seen tumbling
With actions giving reasons to scold

Gauging a war, many say had they seen
Behind the walls, its peculiar smoke haze
Approval's not where their vote would have gone
Ignoring the antics that spiked its craze

A peek inside a window of shame
Attempting to fight wars on one's own
Revelations will surge in a tyrant's behavior
For self-serving decisions made alone

(2004)

Family Setting

The sun sets on a family tree
Where many emotions seem to hide

Daring to say what we hear or see
Much is probably in disguise

To marvel at those who's near and dear
Surprised at the things they do

Watching their habits and daily acts
That seems to get them through

Though the hidden and harbored secrets
Kept silent, most will never admit

All those social and familial shortcomings
That's avoided for being misfits

In doubt of a perfect family tree
On God's earth anywhere

Gives me heartfelt assurance for mine
For which I've found time to care

(2002)

Color Guarded

Behind sunshine, rainbows and cloudy skies
Showers lurked to erase all doubt

On the horizon sat another brewing storm
Of behaviors with little reason to shout

Dramas unfolding before their eyes
Became the thief of family pride

A ceremonial surprise was ushered in
Unveiled and unable to hide

Climbing steep mountains with minor steps
While frivolity is so loose and untamed

A presence reducing many to tears
Was a bittersweet joy mired in shame

Family feelings simmered at most
As acceptance remained lukewarm

The innocence bred in all this drama
Hailed her own demanding charm

Snuggling close to plant a tender kiss
Babbling with truth and wide eyes

Speaking in barely audible mumbles
Verse that only comes from a child

Family feelings slowly began to melt
Unable to hold their joy at bay

For this adorable little bundle of color
Acceptance finally found its way

(1972)

A Fallen Star

She lived a fast and fanciful life
Though very little freedom to move
Events fuelled her latent misery
As she struggled to find her groove

Money, good looks and a determined will
Propelled her to instant fame
She created light wherever she went
As others pleasured her as fair game

The beleaguered fame to which she rose
Empathy assailed upon her rise
Such weighty assets she willingly exposed
All packaged in eye-popping size

A life that never stood so still
Men entitled their playground
They, she thought, were an easy escape
But love from them she never found

(2006)

The Home-Cooked Meal

Accepting a long-standing invitation
At the urging of a treasured friend

The awaited reply to a home-cooked meal
Was "Thank you," or never hear the end

Elusive about what was being served
Wielding powers as a decent cook

A pride in making meals from scratch
She bragged of never using cookbooks

Like any dinner guest, I expected to find
A hot, delicious meal with style

A quiet mood, harmony and a lovely host
Should make any bachelor smile

Anxiously waiting to fill the hunger
For which my stomach cried

To join her over a well-dressed table
And a chance to feast with pride

An honor and privilege to share this meal
At appearance, took much to prepare

But short of cooking lessons and the hunt for a man
Invitations should be few and rare

Steak offered was likely from the mother cow
That could be mistaken for her hide

Said a prayer over fat in collard greens
And peas Mother Nature overdried

An ear of corn adorned my plate
With kernels that failed to plump

With cornbread nearly too stiff to eat
And chocolate pudding with lumps

Black coffee much too strong to drink
And hot chocolate that wouldn't dissolve

A palate for the soul lacking in this feast
Was an ordeal beyond resolve

Be cordial and keep the evening pleasant
I was warned…to make the most

Eat after you leave if you're still hungry
By all means, don't offend the host….

(2002)

The Male Room

When relationships
Are shrouded in lust

Behaviors can become
Complex and unjust

Unfamiliar feelings
Held hostage in a room

Is on a fast course
Of relationship doom

Passes are made
Amid confusions of no

One should leave
But never poised to go

Things get unruly
And out of hand

Someone has made an
Unreasonable demand

Though a whirlwind affair
Things were looking good

Beliefs and intentions
Have been misunderstood

What happened between them
Is anybody's guess

To inappropriate behavior
Neither will confess

(2005)

Stamp of Approval

Bursting at the seams with nature's seeds
A glorious variety fills society's needs

Troubles are breeding and brewing under skin
With an ignorance of the heart's core within

Skin that's pigmented in a variety of tones
Shows the cultural wealth of how we are grown

Men that are tall, skinny, fat and some burly
Hair that's missing, some straight and some curly

Tall women, thin women, some short and round
Too many with a focus on image and pounds

Big eyes, small eyes, round, or maybe slanted
In hues only the Master should have planted

Many shave and sculpt the body for show
By inflating areas that failed to grow

To sign off these traits as nature's mistakes
Let's be wary of rearranging what God makes

Unhinge those judges that need removal
As one hardly needs another stamp of approval

(2004)

A Widow's Haze

Growing frail, Jesse's old familiar face
Is quite charming, with a youthful appeal
Once a beauty of ageless grace
Her assets—time's begun to steal

Bearing scars of a love that abruptly ended
She's seasoned, but beyond quick repair
A broken heart that's in need of mending
Trapped, with those of little to share

Attracting the attention of a younger man
With exploits worn on his sleeve
Whose aim and interest is to yield what he can
In his haze of affection, she's pleased

In their ages, there are calendar lapses
In a battle with loneliness at its peak
Mincing minds and a generation gap
Her senses are rattled and weak

Coveting a love that's merely a token
Her heart has failed to resurrect
Too early for one so ravaged and broken
Lurked a hunger to heal and protect

A jolting emergence from a widow's haze
A voice of reason reigned in this old soul
Loyalists from her past showed up to heal
A heart whose ego took its toll

Age appropriate for crochet and knitting
If again lust raises its ugly head
With Jessie though, crafting is hardly befitting
So for therapy, it's a good book instead

(2004)

Wired

You're off to school, alive and wired
A first year's journey on your own

A time to use wisely while you're away
And ultimately show how you've grown

Resist microwaving all of your meals
Or you will never learn how to cook

And there's nothing wrong with lessons online
If you continue to read your books

A life that's filled with multiple choices
Need wisdom in knowing what to choose

A condensed text is handy at times
But much of the story you could lose

Refrain from abbreviating all of your words
In messages you're dying to send

Realize message clarity is necessary
As shabby spelling is hard to comprehend

Tempted with quick notes when pressed for time
Suggests doing reports in a hurry

Allowing technology to eclipse the mind
It's time that we all start to worry

(2005)

Guarded Passions

The breath of passion in your children
Makes them feel near and dear
Show them how to appreciate life
And make good the purpose they're here

Show passion for our daily freedom
That's so often taken for granted
Learn to protect and share this precious land
Upon whose soil we've been planted

Embrace the passion for human difference
Appreciating the value of every life
By respecting the presence of your fellow man
Without imposing undue strife

(2002)

The Reunion

Tender memories of friends and kin
When we played childhood games
With clapping hands and tapping feet
To a tune of rhyming names

Those wondrous times seek to remind
And reflect what is long outgrown
A tradition classified under happy times
Broken? Or simply a loss of tone

The reality of speed bumps to maturation
A new job or more years in school
Journeyed on a trail of frenzied growth
Of endeavors with a host of new rules

Shedding years of anticipation
Loomed a reunion with a gracious return
Sadly, it was met with little participation
Of a past boding little concern

But a hungering curiosity to venture back
Smacked down any foreboding fear
Of recognizing those overstuffed in frocks
On sisters amassed front and rear

With jocks and hunks now short and round
The mind wandered where the eyes could not
Blind faith was reminisced in old glory
As truth of fiction loomed in earshot

Suspicions of what keeps them coming
As future interest lingers in doubt
Pity that so many failed to outgrow
What time showed left to talk about

(2011)

The Pursuit of Justice

A young man who has been profiled
Just may be holding a grudge

A dancer who has been working all night
May have to be given a nudge

An old man reading the morning news
Still dreams of becoming a judge

An old lady bringing pastries to the crowd
Is more interested in her fudge

A pompous young man pampering his looks
Shows off as rather vain

A harried woman with three small kids
Has a problem just keeping sane

A militant young woman with an attitude
Shows she has an axe to grind

Can they render a verdict that's fair
For the justice they're seeking to find?

It really is no honor when called to duty
For the chance to judge a criminal matter

And linger all day with total strangers
In silence or meaningless chatter

(2006)

Wisdom in the Jungle

Wisdom is golden in a pool of peers
And a nurturing test of one's views
Lurking circumstances can quickly arise
And often hard to undo when others choose

Be wary in following another's lead
To places you've not yet seen
The need for wisdom in the jungle of life
Are planned exits beyond the green

In a forest that's absent of thickets and brush
Despite all directions you're lost
Break with the hunger to follow those
Invitations that carry grave costs

Harness the joy of your own beliefs
And their value as you would any treasure
Know that one's views are mental adventures
Against your own, you take time to measure

(2003)

Truancy

It's never been a
Secret that any child
Was ever in school
By choice

Truancy is a tradition
That lives on today
And forever
Maintains a voice

Parents must impress
Upon their youth
Education's the recipe
For success

Without it
Only brings defeat
And a life filled
With misery and distress

(2007)

Winds of Darkness

Winds of darkness
Ravaging the coast
Whose rolling rage
Has racked the most
Scattering and forcing
Every sprig of life
Its fierce turbulence
Leaving heavy strife

Mother Nature has sent
Her message again
Take cover immediately
Wherever you can
Her winds are in a tantrum
That you cannot match
They'll gnarl and lash
Everything in their path

To watch this tempest
Dancing at sea
Churning, all of its voices
Roaring at me
Such capricious winds
I could never withstand
With its eye upon me
I dare play my hand

(2005)

An Open End

Moms, they say, are taken for granted
So exploits of my behavior you're warned
Though it's all good and well-intentioned
A fair explanation you've earned

I'm back home without reservations
With my music, and still playing it loud
I'm prepared this time to make my own
And someday make you proud

Yes! My domain's always in a mess
Plenty of junk, but valued stuff
There's radar for everything in my world
Under stress you seem to be engulfed

Too much activity on the phone…
I'm just making time with my friends
You and I are within each other's reach
And our time has an open end

You say I listen with a head of steel
A disorder that arouses your pain
Since our minds are no longer in conflict
The harmony in our hearts is attained

(2005)

The Will

The sacred will for the sun to rise
And its promise to return and set

It's the same will for the blinded eyes
To see a light they've never met

Just as this will soothe our aching feet
After walking a metered mile

It reserves grace for the angry mouth
That's badly in need of a smile

The will to clear a clouded mind
When it rambles about in thought

Requires the need for absolute faith
When blessings from God are sought

There's a will to heal a broken heart
That unconditional love will mend

With God's will every girl and boy
Can become strong women and men

(1999)

A Seat at the Table

In the midst of wars I've lost my way
On missions you've ordered me to own
As my life has always been without a country
I am fearless when I meet the unknown

Before this journey I'd like to be able
To examine the reason for this trip
For once just give me a seat at the table
As I prepare to meet the unequipped

You've given me the power to take any land
Undoubtedly many will die in vain
I have no voice…nor do I have a plan
What on this journey am I to gain?

Cultural differences I'm forced to neglect
So there's no chance of common ground
Unleashing me without a hint of respect
Burns any bridge for peace to be found

As a vessel without a heart or brain
You're forcing me to do as I am told
I have no ability beyond causing great pain
By engaging the same wars of old

Before I ruin or destroy another nation
With staggering stealth I know I'm able
We're well beyond building relations
When I cannot have a seat at the table

Wanted: Romance

Desperation clouded Flo's clarity of thought
And she offered up her unarmed heart
In a culture where love's often misguided
It can drive the heart and soul apart

Ambitious designs to raise her odds
Of that rare potential interest of love
Silently in the shadow of this gamble
Lurked a profile as fitting as a glove

Pressures forced her desperate mind
And heart as she shopped for romance
Swept into the arms of a pernicious spirit
Evil arrived ripe for its chance

Leaping without caution into this affair
Trust never had a chance to bloom
Designs requiring that special care
For a heart relinquished too soon

Loneliness lingered beneath anxious desire
Trusting any man should be a must
But distracted under a spell of romantic notions
Character was defeated by lust

A blooming surprise that neither expected
Revealed what her new man couldn't afford
Was his goal to silence a one night affair?
Or betray one he claimed to adore

His dalliances finally landed him squarely
Under a suspicious cloud of fear

To escape his behavior and family disgrace
Flo's misfortune was to disappear

As she lay innocent of abandoned power
The town spoke over her silent rest
Love ones celebrated a curious departure
With prayer for their honored guest

As tears spilled from ninety nine eyes
For lips that's been quietly hushed
Dizzying revelations had ravaged the feelings
Of so many severely bruised and crushed

Was there any wonder about the past?
Of a convincing spirit should have mattered
Or a check of what lurked in his heart
Before setting up so many to be shattered

About the Author

Johnnie Walker was born in Warner Robins, Georgia, where she received her education, graduating as salutatorian of her class. She was always thinking and learning outside the classroom, so college was not an immediate on her radar. She moved to Atlanta and went to work for the IRS. After six months on the job she realized college didn't look so bad. In the summer of '66 she enrolled in a liberal arts program at the University of Tampa, where she excelled in its English language program. She returned to Atlanta and went to work for AT&T then Chubb & Sons but neither company gave her the movement she wanted in her life. Now, it was either college for four years of math, or travel. She chose Delta Air Lines, where she remained for thirty years. After retirement, she went back to work under contract in human resources for Delta. What was supposed to be a four-month assignment turned into three years. One day, while sitting in traffic, she casually whispered, "God, I know there's something else you want me to be doing, so please show me what it is." Three days later, she awakened in early morning with a full poem and an explosion of other ideas. With pen and paper at bedside, she started scribbling. By midmorning she had written twelve poems. She is still writing with another book coming soon.

CPSIA information can be obtained
at www.ICGtesting.com
Printed in the USA
BVHW080947200721
612421BV00006B/144